Discover Yourself

Unleash your inner energy to achieve the purpose of your life!

notionpress.com

Discover Yourself

Unleash your inner energy to achieve the purpose of your life!

Mahatab Mullan

notionpress.com

Notion Press

5 Muthu Kalathy Street, Triplicane,

Chennai - 600 005

First Published by Notion Press 2015

ISBN: 978-93-52060-37-5

This book is dedicated to my husband Xerxes Mullan, who has been very encouraging and supportive throughout my journey of expressing my thoughts and penning it down. He has been a true inspiration. He has also gone through some of the mystical experiences mentioned in this book. I am very grateful and thankful to my late parents, who have always been an inspiration and strength through my life.

Unleash Your Inner Energy to Achieve the Purpose of Your Life!

To me, discover means to discard the cover to reveal the real! Yes! And having said that, how many of us have discovered ourselves? Do you think that if you have not yet discovered yourself, how will others discover you? We all want to be successful, rich, famous and loved, but how is all this possible if we do not know who we are?

Now, let me tell you that when you really achieve something in life and do not know what you want to do with it, you will simply be disappointed. It is like dreaming about a beautiful partner, and when you really get one, you discover that you are bored with the beauty and that you would have appreciated more brains than beauty. That is your discovery, but may be you would have not taken the step to go ahead if you had really discovered what you wanted in the first place through some deep questioning to yourself.

We humans, like computers, are programmed to think in a certain way, behave in a certain way, react in a certain way and eventually become a certain person who we ourselves do not know much about. This conditioning is done by our parents, friends, teachers, family and many, surrounding our lives day in and day out. To an extent, their perception about ourselves becomes reality for us, which is not the real you or closest to the truth of who you are.

Let me tell you a story about an eagle that discovered how to fly. Now, you would think what stupidity is this? Eagles not only fly, but they also fly really high! So, the story goes like this: There was an eagle that laid an egg, and unfortunately got killed by a hunter. Now, the egg somehow landed up in a chicken's nest with other chicken eggs. Later, when all the eggs were hatched, there were small chicks that came out including the baby eagle. The mother chicken was a little suspicious about the baby eagle, but as time went by the baby eagle became very attached to mama chicken and the other baby chickens.

They all looked like one big happy family. Eventually, the baby eagle would become stronger and bigger day by day with large wings, while the baby chicks grew up to be delicate and small. However, just to fit in with the group, the eagle; who was now fully grown, never dared to discover his true self. Until, one day, another eagle came by to kill one of the chickens. The eagle became very protective about them and picked up a fight with the intruding eagle.

The fight was intense and continued for long, until the eagle managed to win over the intruder. The mother chicken was watching the fight all along, but she always knew that the eagle was not her child. However, she never let him know for she was afraid that he would discover himself and that they would lose out on a good protector. The intruder told the eagle just one thing before he left that transformed his life: "I don't understand. You are a very strong eagle, and if you choose to, you can rule the eagle clan of this forest. Then, why are you behaving like a chicken?"

These harsh words hit the eagle very hard. He was in shock when he asked the intruder, "Does that mean I can fly as high as you?" The intruder said in a mocking tone, "With the kind of wings you have, you can fly higher than me, but only if you choose to and willing to have faith in yourself that you can do it". Saying this, the intruder left not realising the impact he had left on the eagle.

The eagle was at first in a denial mode, and it took a lot of courage to confront his so-called mother chicken who had no option but to tell him the truth. Even after he listened to the truth, the eagle was not willing to let go of the chicken family where he was comfortable and happy. But the mother chicken knew that the time had come to let go of him so that he could discover the freedom by himself. The entire chicken family reassured him continuously to make him believe that the jungle was out there waiting for him and that he should leave and fly off as he belonged to the jungle and not the farm.

With perseverance and realisation, the eagle for the first time flew off and never returned. He had ultimately discovered who he was and what it takes to be free!

Now, how many of us have always tried to fit in with the herd? Meaning, our friends are going to a party and I must also go there tonight; all my friends have registered for so and so classes, I must also register to the same classes; everybody in my school wants to join this college and I would also love to do it; my colleague in office wears this brand, so I also want it irrespective of how I look in it; she has planned for her retirement, so I have to also do it.

He is doing it, so I also want to do it! She is doing that, so I also want to do it! He/she has opted for a specific career and making good money, I also need to do it irrespective of whether I like it or not! What we do not realise is that we are always following and not giving enough thought to what we really like to do or who we are. We just want to copy, not realising that we are unique individuals with very different sets of talents that we need to discover and excel in to find the ultimate freedom.

I am an avid lover of art and during my younger days, when I used to see a piece of art and compare it to other art pieces, to my amusement some of the art pieces were priced exorbitantly as compared to others. To add to my anxiety, they were not as good as the others, yet most of them had sold-out tags attached. So, I would keep asking the question "why so?" to equally ignorant friends, who gave me unsatisfactory answers and avoided further discussion. A few years later, I discovered that these paintings were originals and that the others were reproductions (i.e., either the idea was not original or it lacked uniqueness, etc.). So, I realised that there were few buyers of reproductions and more for original art, and did not mind paying a premium for it.

So here too, people around would still not stop copying or aping others. This is because our educational system does not encourage us to think but *to do* a lot. As a result, doing a lot puts pressure on individuals, who then come up with an easy way out – copying. I do not blame them, as history has proved that we humans were monkeys before we evolved as humans, and the DNA of copying seems to have been stuck with many of us; only a few have evolved in the true sense!

This is so true to an extent that if you show your friend some wonderful piece of work, he would probably look at you with his pupil dilated, asking you, "Have you done this yourself?" To which you would answer, "Yes". He would promptly reply, "Really?" You would again say, "Yes". Then, with a mocking look on his face, he would say, "I don't believe you! You are lying aren't you?" Now, you would say, "No, this is my work". He would not leave you, "Come on, you must have got this idea from somewhere". This would lead to a war of words trying to convince your friend that this really is your original piece of work and that you have not copied. But the monkey brain that he is just does not get it, which is in constant denial mode. It is not his fault that the monkey brain does not allow him to think straight. So, we all need to ask a question: Can we evolve in our thought process? Can we do some deep thinking of who we are? What is my purpose? What am I good at? What we love doing that others appreciate and are willing to pay a price for it? These questions, no doubt, look very easy but very difficult to find an answer for.

Now, I do not have an answer for all the questions. As I mentioned earlier, each one of us are unique individuals with different sets of talents that we are born with or have the ability to develop it, so that we can find answers to most of the questions. Similarly, our goals and purpose in life is also very different, as each of us are unique individuals. It is not possible to give you one path/solution that suits or solves all your problems. So, what I am going to do is take you through a journey with me to explore yourself and dig deep into yourself to find the real you, and take you through instances, stories with underline meanings, preaching's from powerful people and my real-life instance to make this journey a pleasurable one! The journey is going to be exhaustive, long and bumpy. But if you have the perseverance and belief, you will make it. However, in this journey, one needs patience – I mean, if there is some instance or story that you can relate to or has touched your inner cord, then please stop there and introspect as this could the point or your true moment of discovering yourself.

Also, you will probably ask me a question: why should I take pains to discover myself? I am alright doing whatever I am doing right now; I also know that nobody around me cares and neither do I, as far as I am doing well in all aspects of my life. To which I would say, "You definitely have a point here, but now let me ask you a few questions to ponder. All is well now, but what happens if it is not in the future? Are you equipped to handle a tough situation ahead of you? What if you are diagnosed with cancer or any other terminal diseases? What if you lose your job and nobody is willing to hire you and you have bills to pay every month? What if you lose your dear ones too soon? You can have control over yourself, but how can you control the situation around you?"

However, I do not have answers to any of the questions, but I can assure you that if you believe in discovering yourself you would be well equipped to handle the situation much better and, in some cases, you would be able to protect yourself from these instances of having occurred in your life. You would then ask as to how you know what the future holds for you and what is the proof that one can evade all the undesirable situations? To which, also, I do not have an answer; but after you have practiced the techniques thoroughly that I am about to reveal, you will be able to look around and at least say that you are by far much better off than most of your colleagues, friends, relatives, neighbors and so on. I can also assure you that you would find tremendous joy within you and would like to live your life all over again!

So, if you are ready to travel that journey where you would find innate harmony, peace and happiness in all spectrums of your life, please do read on.

First, I would like to thank you for having belief in me and a positive outlook towards the life transformation process. I would urge you to read this book carefully to understand the underlying meaning of what is being said, and I promise you that I will keep the language as simple as possible to ensure that you have only my book in front of you and not distracted by the *Oxford Dictionary* for any reference.

Now that I have your undivided attention, I will start at the grass root level. First, I want you to believe that no two humans are the same and that each human has a specific purpose and goal to achieve before he/she leaves this planet. I would substantiate my belief by saying that though most of us are blessed with two eyes, ears, hands and legs, one head, nose, mouth and so on, and our organs perform same functions like listening, seeing, hearing, eating, digesting, defecating and so on, we as human are very different from others. For example, music which may be melodious to my ears may be very irritating to you; or the food which I love, you may not want to see the sight of it; the person whom I have fallen in love with, you may dislike the person so much that you would even think twice about considering him as a friend.

Why is it that one person loves something and the other hates it equally? Which part of our body accepts and which rejects? Some of you would say mind, while some may say heart. But listen to this: is it the heart that accepts/rejects or is it the thought that accepts/rejects? Here, I would want you to recall a famous proverb "Love is blind". Now, let us say that when a person does not have vision, how will mind or heart accept/reject? In reality, they do accept and reject with their other senses. Now, between all senses, mind and heart, there has to be a connection. A connection that is mysterious. A connection not fully explained by anyone. Some may say that it is a gut feeling, while others may say it is the soul that ultimately decides.

Whatever the belief, one thing is certain – there is an intangible energy within each of us. An energy that we are blessed with, an energy that we feel, an energy that is powerful, an energy that cannot be destroyed, an energy that connects us, an energy that can make or break us and an energy that resides within us that is constantly changing our thoughts. It is an energy that controls us all the time, an energy which neither grows old nor dies; it only travels, and yet most of us are so oblivious to this energy within us.

One can never see this energy, we can only feel it. Some of the most powerful energies on earth cannot be seen. Can you see the electromagnetic waves or the network frequency waves? Can you see gravity? Yet, they do such amazing things in our lives, and hence this universe is full of powerful energies. Some of the powerful energies are positive, and to balance them there are negative energies, as well. The reason I am explaining this is we are a part of this energy. And, it is very important to understand the whole part first, in order to understand the part of the whole. It is like when you join an organisation, they first make you aware of the organisational goals and vision, and later tell you to align your goals with the organisational goals in order to make the organisation prosper and achieve its goals.

However, it is not that simple to understand this humungous mysterious energy of the universe like an organisational goal. Nevertheless, all our energies are a tiny part of this mammoth energy. So, the way I look at it is very simple – look within yourself first and then try to look outside. To start with, try to first uncover your energy, understand it and study it, and then mould it to attract favourable external energy required to shape your future to fulfill the ultimate purpose. To some, this may sound like Greek and Latin, but I assure you that it is only when you read with belief, you will soon see your life changing for good.

I strongly believe that we are a part of a whole and we still are very different because if that was not true, then all of us would just be like one. All of us would have only one goal and all of us would be equally talented. To substantiate further, why is it that some of us are good at art while others good at numbers? some of us are very good in sports, while some very good at drama; some love to paint, while some love to write; some love to travel, while others like to stay at home. But, in all this diversity, there is unity, harmony, peace, abundance, balance and love. Specifically balance, because there is never an instance where every human being wants just one thing or wants to become successful in just one profession. Imagine if all of us have the talent and would want to paint, paint and paint all the time! Then, who will do the other work? How will human race survive? There would be utter chaos and there would be only misery and disharmony on this planet.

Individual energies are like pieces of jigsaw puzzle. We need to fit in so well that one can see the bigger picture. Imagine a big jigsaw puzzle has some pieces missing or the puzzle has some pieces that do not fit. How would it finally look? It will look incomplete, right? Now, if we do not align our energies with others, we will never achieve completeness. Remember, we were taught in schools that humans are a social being and that we need to socialise. Why is that? Why do we feel so good about our near and dear ones? Sometimes we feel a strong connection, while sometimes there is a repulsive feeling with some people? There is a definite connection with people around us, the energies match and sometimes one can draw energies from others. So, if you hang around with positive people, you are likely to draw positive energy and same is true vice versa.

At times, we think of a person and the phone rings. Guess what? The person whom we were thinking of is on the phone. We call it coincidence because we are unable to explain the phenomenon. Why do we feel unrest at times when our dear ones are in danger even if we are thousands of miles away? This is because we are connected by an invisible energy. This is the energy that we cannot see but feel strongly. Well, we can feel that some of our connections are very strong, while with others it is weak. Again, all of us do not feel it if our own energy is dormant and not awake, and we are not conscious of it. One has to tune into the energy frequency like we tune into a radio frequency to listen. It is not easy to listen to our own and others' energy, as it requires a lot of meditation and constant practice. Nevertheless, it is achievable.

Each of us has a unique energy with different intensity in order to fulfill our goals successfully. And, it is this energy that drives us to do what we do. However, some of us have dormant energy which needs to be activated in order to achieve the desired goal. While some of us do not allow the energy within us to stay dormant, we continuously draw strength and courage from it to achieve our purpose quicker than others. And, yet some of us not only use our internal energy, but also draw energy from the cosmic world to achieve phenomenal results. One person is Albert Einstein, who was a genius and some believed that he achieved his great work by drawing energy from the external cosmic world to become a genius on this planet.

Sometimes, the dormant energy is invoked and it performs miracles. Yes, miracles do happen! Have we all not heard about so and so in his late 50s who had transformed his life and now he is a totally new person? This person is more composed, more evolved, more successful and definitely happier, and now ready to take on the world! How did this change happen? Even if one would ask this question to this newly evolved human, he would exclaim that something within him changed, there was this inner deep-down voice that guided him and he just followed what he felt strongly. A classic example was Gautama Buddha, who one fine day left everything to follow his inner voice. However, this does not happen to everybody, it happens to very few. Are we going to be one of them is the question to ponder upon.

A lot of you must have wondered many times – why is it that some people are born talented? But have you ever wondered – we are all born talented, but some of us have to yet discover our talent. And even if we do not have the inbuilt talent, we have the ability to develop it if we want to and excel in any field we have a passion for. Also, a lot of us have wondered that though he/she is talented in a specific field, why is he/she not putting in his/her best effort for the greatest outcome? But have we ever thought that may be the individual purpose would be very different from what he/she wants to achieve and that they still need to unearth their true purpose in life of what they want to be.

Is it not true that many a times you are good at doing something, but your interest level is very low? Your internal energy is just not aligned to do that, even though you may have the talent for it. That is truly the indication of you not having discovered yourself, yet. Have you not felt of doing some work which does not feel right? This is nothing to do with where, how or to whom you are born. You know a lot of times we ask why? Why do I have to do this or why do I have to do that? Why am I like this or why am I like that? Why do I have to go through all this or that? But how many of us have ask the question to ourselves that why am I here? What is my purpose? Perhaps, some of us did ask this question, but have we really asked and looked into ourselves deeply to unearth the truth?

How many of us do what we are doing and have found immense pleasure, joy and peace in what we are doing? When a true artist paints, he forgets everything around him and is so engrossed in his painting that he achieves a meditative state, and when he comes out of it he is amazed by his own creation. How many of us have immersed ourselves into our work and have found immense happiness? So much so that, when we do what we enjoy doing, we forget everything and anything, including time.

I am a Zoroastrian, and one of the rituals performed during a funeral is that a dog is brought in where the deceased is laid. There are various benefits obtained through this ceremony. One of them is to make certain that the person is really dead, and dogs are believed to detect signs of life that a human might miss. This is really intriguing, as there have been cases where the doctors have declared the person dead but the dog has managed to prove them wrong, as the dog was able to sense the energy of the person to be alive! Though scientifically it is not proven as to what does the dog actually sniff? Is it the heartbeat? Or is it the brain wave? Or is it something else? But think about it – if doctors have clinically declared him dead, it means all his critical life organs are dead. So, what does that leave us with? Do you get it now?

It is the energy within a person which has not yet left the body. The energy that refuses to leave the body and wants the body to come back to life to fulfill its purpose or it could be that the energy is taking a bit longer to leave the body but eventually escapes after deliberations.

Dogs are known to sniff vibes, which are nothing but the waves of energy within us. If our energy within is not positive, then the dog would immediately sniff it. So, you be aware of that. It should be noted here that if the energy is extremely dormant, then even the dogs would not be able to sniff it. There is deep awakening an individual has to do if their energy level is dormant in order to activate it. This requires lot of effort and constant cleansing.

Sometimes, our energy within us connects with the cosmic energies for help without us being aware. It is then that the cosmic energies have their mysterious ways to shake us up. The jolt given by the cosmic energy is very intense at times, a sudden unexplained experience in our lives. It is like someone trying to tell you to change. Change for good, change for betterment, change for the purpose we are born for on this planet and change for the ultimate goal to be achieved in order to be in sync with the greater source of the universal energy.

As I write this book, the thoughts just follow and they come to me with ease, and the experience is absolutely effortless. It is like the energy within me is encouraging me to write this and is telling me that I am on the right path. And as I write this in the wee hours of the morning, there is some kind of peace within me which resonates with the cosmic energy. This cannot be explained, as it is not very simple. It can only be experienced! Now that I am aware of the energy within me, I listen to it very carefully to take any major decisions; I know it will never let me down and will always support me for all the right things that I do.

Having said that let me give you a small example. When I was looking to buy my first house, I saw many houses, almost close to a hundred. To my amusement, I was not able to explain to the agents why I did not like a particular house which had all the criteria that I had explained to them. One thing which I was never able to put across in a way they would get it was the energy type and level. I would reiterate to them that the energy has to be good in the house I am buying. They would give me a blank stare and say that you check it yourself when you visit the house. Later, I decided that this was something that could not be explained as to what I wanted in a few short words, so I continued to go through the torture of visiting endless number of houses with the agents. You would, of course, ask me that all along I was talking about the energy within us, now what am I talking about? Let me explain. When an individual stays in a particular place for a long time, their energies is exposed to the energy around them. In the process, they emit certain vibes that surround the environment, and some of it also remains in it. So, what I experience at times is that there was negative energy in some houses, while there was positive energy in others but they were in a dormant state. The reason I did not want to buy these houses was that they would only harm my level of energy. Let me give you an analogy here. Say, for instance, if you stay with people who have cold, there is going to be a high probability you would also catch a cold! It is something like that! If you surround yourself with an environment that has low or negative energy, there is high possibility that your energy level will try to match theirs, and very soon it will dominate the energy within you.

My quest for buying the appropriate house continued, and in the process the agents were amused as I turned down some very good offers which were termed as "hot cakes", but I turned them all down as they did not meet the criteria that I was looking for. Finally, I stumbled upon a cute apartment and immediately my face brightened. With a sigh of relief, I told myself, "Whoa! This is it! I found it". The experience of stepping into my now-acquired apartment was amazing. It was as if the energy over there was waiting to welcome me. It enveloped me as if telling me I am not going to let you down. I, then, quickly made the down payment and went ahead with the registration. Finally, the apartment was mine.

Honestly, at that time I could not afford that apartment as I had to pay monthly installment to the bank for the money I had borrowed. So, I put it up for rent. Here again, I was very particular about whom I gave my apartment for rent. There was never a problem getting tenants. Most of them loved my small cozy apartment, and to my amusement all the tenants who stayed in my apartment prospered and became very happy! So much so that some of them also offered to buy my apartment and were also willing to pay premium for it. I understood that it is not the apartment, it is the energy within that is doing the miracle.

Not only did the tenants gain positive experiences in their lives, but I too gained prosperity, wealth and happiness. Some say it is the house that brought me luck, but I believed that my energy attracted this positivity in my life! Let me explain. When our energy level is very positive and active, there is a certain amount of restlessness and the vibes are so strong that it attracts other energies. Though unlike magnet that attracts opposites, our energies attract all types of energies but favour the energy type we already have. Have we not had the experience that when we meet someone for the first time, we feel as if we have known the person for long time and feel happy about it? This is because our energies match, attract and draw these people to us. All who come into our lives have a purpose and they only facilitate to achieve our goals in life. However, you may wonder how people with negative energy facilitate us to achieve our goals.

They do it in a way that you may not be aware of. For example, there have been instances wherein a negative person may give you a lot of stress at work so that you do not succeed. You get very frustrated and quit, only to realise you have loads of potential and that you could become a partner in a business, which eventually becomes very successful. I have experienced this phenomenon, and can be true for others, too, in many ways. Sometimes, these negative people may try to harm you, but remember that because of them you could also get closer to positive people, wherein you get a good friend for life who would help you achieve your purpose. So, good or bad, positive or negative people come and go in our lives but it is up to us to leverage them in order to achieve our purpose.

Till now, I have explained some basic concepts of our inner energy and how it can help us achieve our ultimate purpose, happiness, peace, success and so on and so forth. I will now explain further a few steps we should take to have our energy active and positive, because without this it is extremely difficult to achieve what we want in life.

Contents

Chapter 1

Drop Dead

If you ask me whether I need to die to achieve my purpose, I would say “No”! Drop dead – not in the literal sense. Let me explain this with a small story. Once upon a time, there was a trader from the United Kingdom, who visited India for trading purpose. On his way to work, he saw some colorful parrots in a beautiful park. The parrots were so pretty that he could not help but get drawn to them. When he reached very close to them, he was taken aback as they were not only very pretty but were also able to talk to each other in his language (i.e., English). He was so fascinated that he started a conversation with them, and was extremely ecstatic about it. It was then that he decided he would take one of them with him as a companion as he did not have anybody in his life to talk to. So, he offered the most handsome looking parrot to accompany him back home and he promised him that he would be very happy in his home country. The parrot somehow agreed to travel with him to the United Kingdom.

The trader was very excited about taking the parrot home. When he reached home with the parrot, he thought that it would not be safe to let the parrot roam around freely. So, he bought a big cage, decorated it as beautifully as he could, and then let the parrot in and closed the cage door. He also bought some delicious meals for the parrot, which the parrot had never eaten before. The parrot relished the food and was very happy, as he no more had to go searching for food, water or shelter. The trader, in turn, was also very happy as the parrot happened to be good company for him. As days, weeks and months passed by, both the trader and the parrot were very happy because the parrot was taken good care of and the trader never felt lonely again.

Later, the trader had to visit India again for his business. He remembered that India was the place where he had got this beautiful talking parrot from. However, as he was visiting India, he thought it would be a good idea to carry any message that the parrot would like to convey to his near and dear ones. With this in mind, he approached the parrot to inform him that he would be travelling to India the next day and that if he wanted to he could send some message to his near and dear ones. The parrot told the trader to tell all his family members and friends that he is extremely happy to be here and that he has never been this happy before, as he has a very good caretaker who gives him all the exotic food, drinks and shelter. Additionally, he is also very good company to have around.

The trader was very happy to hear that and he promised the parrot that he would indeed visit his family and friends to give the message, and that if they had any messages, in turn, would pass that on to him when he returned. Next day, the trader left for India and as promised, he visited the same park where the parrot had lived with his family and friends. When he reached the very spot as last time, all the parrots gathered around him as they recognised him and wanted to know about their friend back in the United Kingdom. The trader wished all of them and told them that he had a message for them from the parrot. They eagerly asked him what was it, to which the trader replied that he has told me to tell you all that he is extremely happy in the United Kingdom and that he has a beautiful cage to live in and that he gets to eat all the exotic food that he had never eaten before and also the trader kept him in good company. After listening to this, one of the parrot's pupils dilated and within a few seconds dropped dead. All the parrots gathered around him. The trader was socked and he inquired as to what had happened. One of them replied, "Sir, he was a very good friend of the parrot whom you had taken to the United Kingdom. He has been in a shock and now he is dead!"

The trader inquired as to the cause of his sudden death? To which they replied that they had no idea. After listening to this, the trader was intrigued by the way the parrot died in such a mysterious way. He kept thinking about it on the whole journey back to the United Kingdom and how would he break this news to the parrot waiting back home. The traveler returned home upset and gathered his courage to break the news to the parrot. But, before he could utter a word, the parrot asked him, "Did you manage to visit my friends and family and give them my message?" The trader replied, "Yes, I did and they were very happy to hear that. But I also have sad news for you". The parrot queried, "What is it? Please tell me all about it and please don't hide anything from me." The trader gathered his courage before breaking the news. "After I finished giving your message, there was this close friend of yours who came forward, stared at me and then just dropped dead!"

After listening to this, the parrot told the trader with great sadness, "You should have sprinkled some water on him immediately to revive him. If you had done it within 10 seconds, there would have been good chances of his survival." To which the trader responded, "I didn't know about it, otherwise I would have definitely done it to save his life." A few seconds later, the parrot stared at the trader and asked, "Do you know the reason of his death?" The trader replied, "No." As soon as he heard the reply, the parrot's pupil dilated and he dropped dead exactly the same way as his friend in India did. The trader was shocked. He immediately opened the cage, removed the parrot from the cage, laid him out on the table and rushed to get some water. On his return, he was shocked to see that the parrot was not on the table. He looked around to see where the parrot had disappeared to.

The parrot shouted from a tree branch just outside the trader's house. When the trader heard the voice, he rushed out and was amazed to see the parrot in perfect health. The trader asked "Why did you drop dead? What happened to you and are you fine now?" To which the parrot replied, "I am in perfect health!" The trader responded, "So, what had happened to you? Please tell me." The parrot replied, "You had just given a very important message from my very dear friend from India." The trader was confused "Me? I gave you a very important message? What is it?

Please, please tell me I can't wait to hear it." The parrot was silent for a moment and then replied, "My best friend sent a message through you that if you want to live your life freely, you need to drop dead!" The trader was shocked; he could not find any words to express himself. He sadly asked the parrot, "So, you are going to leave me and not come back?" To which the parrot nodded and said, "You are right, bye-bye". And the parrot flew high and as fast as he could in the jungle and never returned.

Now you ask yourself how many of you are living a life similar to this parrot when he was in a cage. We get happy with the work we do, the pay we get, the food and the place we live in, and eventually become so complacent that we think and believe that this is what we were meant to become. It is alright; we are not happy doing our work at times, because at the end of every month we get a pay cheque through which we can pay all our bills; it is alright to sacrifice our family lives and not be with them when they need us the most, as we have a very important meeting to attend; It is ok to miss a funeral or two of our near ones, as we were busy travelling for business that we did not really like so much. But our pay cheques have to come in by the end of every month.

To some, these reasons are fine as they are very busy and too involved in their work. But honestly, ask yourself whether you will value any of your business meetings and trips when you are on your death bed. Think about it. Are we all in an auto-pilot mode of surviving and not living our lives the way we are supposed to live? Is doing endless hard work with no interest in it make us programmed robots or humans? We all go through the roller coaster ride in our lives to realise one fine day, "Hey, this is not me. I was not meant to do this", as our inner voice succeeds in taking us over and detest what we continue to do. Do we have time to pause and reflect that is this the life that I want to lead till the end of my time?

In today's fast-moving world, we get caught up in our busy schedules. Even if we get an inner call, which I am sure most of you must have experienced, we would have preferred to give a deaf ear to it as we have reached too far in our lives to stop and start all over again. It sounds horrifying to people to start all over again as they are scared to lose whatever little they have built for themselves. How can we give up and start all over again?

For a moment, think about it. Is it not possible that when the race of life actually started you ran in the opposite direction and that you would never reach the finishing point no matter how hard you tried? In order to finish the race successfully, you have to begin all over again from the starting point! Get back to the days when you were a toddler. Did you not stumble and fall? Did you not get up again to take another step, in other words start all over again? It is painful, no doubt, and the pain lasts for a short period of time. But if you do not pause, step back and start again, you will have to lead a painful journey throughout your life. Now, what is better? Take your pick.

It's like you driving a car endlessly only to discover that you have reached a dead end. Now, will you not stop and reverse your car? Life is very similar and it is never too late. We have to listen to our inner energy, we have to stop all that we are doing and start afresh. Do you not believe in me still? Okay. Let me tell you a story about my friend, who was very passionate about what he was doing. So, he decided to open his own company and within no time his business flourished. He worked very hard day and night, and as his business grew, he hired more people. But because of the rapid growth of his business, he did not invest much time in selecting the right talent which was not good for the company. As a result, he hired the wrong kind of people in key positions. There came a point when he was in conflict with his inner energy, which told him time and again to slow down, pause and reflect which he ignored. Finally, the moment arrived when his business incurred heavy losses. This so shocked him that he eventually invoked his inner energy to rescue him from the situation.

The strong feeling that he experienced urged him to scale down his business immediately to ground zero. He first resisted this thought, but deep down he knew that maybe this was the solution to the problem. Finally, he scaled down his business to ground zero. There was only one person running his company – himself. By doing this, all the customers came back to him as he had a fantastic relationship with them, and his business once again grew from ground zero to a flourishing company. But, this time around, he was very careful in who he recruited into his business. When he did this, he not only saved money, but also got back on track. However, in some cases, the scenario could be totally different, wherein a person is in a profession which he does not love and no desire to work but somehow managing to fare well. In that case, "drop dead" would mean to stop what you are doing and start afresh. Do what you love and enjoy doing it, after listening to your inner voice!

Just as a snake sheds its skin which is dead to embrace the new one, we too must drop dead and start a new life which is willing to embrace us with peace, love, success and happiness.

Chapter 2

Take Good Care of Yourself and the Surroundings

As I had explained earlier, the inner energy is about vibes. If you are surrounded by clutter, then the energies would get clogged and remain dormant. There would be no space for the universal or cosmic energy to not only flow into your surroundings, but the energy within you would also tend to be dormant, which is not good for you. In order to attract positive and active energy from the universe, one has to keep the surroundings very clean and neat. In some cases, wherein your inner self has good energy and is in the process of drawing external energy, the external energy would flow in but will exit fast as the environment is not conducive for it to stay.

For example, when you have guests at home, and if your house is clean and inviting, the probability of the guest staying for a longer time would be high. The same is true for a reversed situation (i.e., if the house is shabby and not clean, then the guest would likely vacate as soon as possible). Have you ever thought about why all the religious places are kept very clean? Why do lots of people visit religious places? What is termed as God is nothing but the highest level of positive energy that has powers to control the universe, and by far the most favourable energy for humans. People go to religious places to draw energy, to invoke their own inner energy.

Religious places everywhere are clean and special prayers recited so that it can pursue the external energy to flow into the holy place. People who visit these religious places have the opportunity to feel it and in some cases absorb it. I have felt the high positive energy vibrations each time I visit a holy place. My inner energy always gets invoked by this energy and I feel very good about it.

However, the opposite is true for attracting negative energy from the universe. In India, some people are known to perform black magic, which is nothing but drawing negative energy from the cosmic world to perform negative activities. This is done in a very dark room, which is not very clean. Generally, the rituals are performed at night or after sunset. This energy is also very powerful and can destroy an individual completely.

Our elders advise us to always go to the holy places after having a head-to-toe bath and with clean clothes. This is because we want to attract positive vibes. This is all about external cleanliness, like wearing clean clothes, keeping our body clean and keeping our surroundings clean and clutter free; but what is also important is keeping our inner body clean.

Keeping our inner body clean means to increase the intake of fruits and vegetables, and reduce poultry, fish, and meat. This is because when we consume a lot of non-vegetarian food (e.g., lamb), then the energy which the lamb had in the past is passed on to us. This energy is mainly negative. Imagine what feelings and vibrations a lamb must have gone through when he/she knew that it was going to be slaughtered. The lamb would be going through a series of emotions like fear, anger, anguish, scared, sad, helplessness and many more. Certainly, you would not want to get all this into your system as it acts like a virus in a computer that would spoil all the programming in a jiffy. This negative energy affects your own energy levels and makes you angry, scared, sad, fearful, helpless and so on, and this only deters you to achieve what your purpose is in this life. In short, it makes your life full of difficulties and challenges.

However, you would argue that all people on this planet who have achieved their purpose are not vegetarians. You are right! They are not! But to reach where they have and to arrive where they have has not been very smooth ride for them either. They would have gone through lot of struggle and hardships before they achieved what they have so far. It is definitely not impossible for individuals to achieve their purpose in life with their inner energy if they are meat eaters, but all I am saying is they had to go through a difficult route to achieve their ultimate goal!

Research has also proved that people who eat a lot of non-vegetarian food are prone to diseases and die faster compared to the vegetarians. Now, do you not think time is at your disadvantage if you are eating poultry, meat, fish and so on day in and day out? It is like if you have to cross a river and you have the option of taking a boat or swim your way across to the other side. It is your choice to pick an option. Irrespective of the options taken, you would make it to the other side. But there may be a possibility that by choosing to swim across, the chances are much lesser that you would make it, as there would be lots of challenges like wild life in the water, you have to be a real good swimmer to reach the other side and so forth.

Imagine you have to take a dive in the sea and you are tied with a big rock. How will you reach the surface, even if you are a very good swimmer? Similarly, all the negative energies like fear, sadness, anger and so on that enters your system through the dead animals, poultry and fish are going to be harmful for yourself. And these energies hinder your path that your inner energy is built for and needs to achieve its ultimate purpose. Why would you like to dig your own grave? Imagine your body to be like a super model. The very best and having the very best – would you not like to feed the very best with the very best? Why would you like to fasten its deformation by feeding all the so-called junk food? Do you not think that only the best and the very best should get into the system? Because our precious energy stays there and if all the negative elements is bogged down, how do you expect it to evolve? How do you expect it to ignite? How do you expect it to be vibrant? It will only give back what it receives and resides in like sadness, fear, helplessness, anger and all the stuff not good for you at all. So, the next time you come across non-vegetarian food, simply turn away and reach out for fresh and healthy vegetarian food.

The fresh and hygienic food will not only keep your body fit and healthy, but it would also make a perfect environment for your energy to evolve and, in turn, help you transform into a new you!

Let me tell you a story. Once there lived a father and his five-year-old son, who was very curious and questioned each and everything around him. Once he asked his dad, “Who lives within us and what is it that makes us”? To which the dad replied, “Son, in each one of us there is a devil and angel who reside within us”. The son was amused at the answer, and asked his dad, “What do they feed on?” To which father replied, “The angel feeds on love, positivity, caring, honesty, unity, passion, kindness etc., while the devil feeds on anger, negativity, fear, dishonesty, insecurity, and cruelty”. “So, since both of them don’t get along, they must be constantly fighting, right?” Father replied, “You are absolutely right son and you know the stronger one would win and eventually you would turn like him”. The son was further intrigued, and he promptly asked his father, “Father, so who eventually would win?” To which the father whispered in his sons ears, “The one you feed the most!”

Our energy within also has the tendency to change from positive to negative and vice versa. It only depends on what we do to ourselves and which energy we feed the most to grow (I will discuss this topic a little later in detail), as our energies not only get affected by the type of food we eat, but also by our surroundings, our thoughts and our friends.

Additionally, abstain from alcohol, smoking or any abusive substances. Refraining from these elements not only keeps you mentally and physically healthier, but also helps any damage being done to our energy. When one consumes alcohol, it is like consuming acid. The acid would have a burning effect on the inner energy. Similarly, smoking is like fire, which also burns everything that comes in its way. You would scoff at this, because most of the successful people are chain smokers or heavy drinkers! But here we are not only talking about success, we are also talking about being a person to fulfill his/her purpose on this planet. These are two different things, as an evolved person is always successful; however, a successful person may not the evolved. Also, a successful person may not be happy, but an evolved person is always happy. While a successful person may not remain successful throughout his/her life, an evolved person will always be successful and will be remembered by the world at large.

To my mind, Gautama Buddha, Mahatma Gandhi, Albert Einstein are some of the evolved human beings. They have not only helped themselves, but the world has also benefitted from them. Buddha was the spiritual guru, Mahatma Gandhi a revolutionary political leader and Albert Einstein a genius scientist. Each one very different, but all served the world in their own different ways. And, of course, there are many, many more, but these three names are on top of my mind.

Though Albert Einstein was not a vegetarian, he once said, "So I am living without fats, without meat, without fish, but am feeling quite well this way. It always seems to me that man was not born to be a carnivore". Gandhi was a strict vegetarian. From a spiritual perspective, Gandhi considered non-vegetarian food and intoxicating drinks abhorrent, as it acted as deterrents to man's inner self-purification and spiritual evolution.

Buddhism has five percepts – not to kill, steal, commit adultery, lie or take any intoxicating substance. However, Buddha did have meat, but that was not by choice. As per Buddhism, they could not buy their own food – they had to eat what others would give them as alms. One day, Buddha was visited by a wealthy person who had a turkey farm. As he was happy after spending time with Buddha, he said that after returning to his farm he would send a feast that would comprise of one of his finest turkey. To which Buddha refused and said he was against killing of any being and that it was not appropriate to do so. Buddha exclaimed, "How one can happily feast by killing a living being?" This clearly proves that Buddha was against eating non-vegetarian food throughout his life.

Now, do not get me wrong. I am really not telling you to quit non-vegetarian food completely. But what I do believe in is that eating too much of it can make it more difficult to use your inner energy more effectively for the greater purpose in life.

Chapter 3

Your Mind – One of the Most Powerful Organs in Your Body

We all know about the famous saying – "As you sow, so shall you reap". But what I really believe is if you sow what your core energy is yearning for, you would reap multi-fold! Yes, I mean it. Let me explain how it is possible. We need to get our mind power to align with our inner core energy and if we are able to do it successfully, then half of our battle is won! But if our mind and core energy are not aligned, then there may be chaos, as you may be successful if you sow some wonderful stuff in your mind and do all the positive affirmations day in and day out to make it happen, and eventually there is high possibility you will be successful as well; but you will soon realise that with great success there will also be a great fall, and the fall will be so fast and steep that before you even realise it you are finished.

Now, think hard and ask yourself as to how did this happen? The answer is – this has happened because there is a conflict between who you are versus who you professed to be. The failure happened because you tried to copy someone versus being original. You failed and not able to bounce back quickly because you were not meant to do that and your energy within has not given you the consensus. You have fallen and do not know how to get back is because you do not love doing it or do not have a passion for it. If you loved what you were doing, then your energy would have given you the strength and courage to bounce back with great vengeance, dedication, skill and knowledge, and you would once again be successful.

But if your energy is not aligned with your mind to do the work, then you would always feel disconnected and the outcome would not be world class. It will not touch the hearts of many. It would at best be good pieces of work, which you would not be able to pursue further as it would mean constant pressure on your mind and suppressing the inner energy flow.

As I write this, I am not certain if I am able to get through to you or whether I am making any sense here. Let me give you an example to make my point clearer. Imagine a high-tech process unit, which churns out a high-quality product each time the process unit is switched on and raw material is fed in. Here, the raw material can be our thoughts, power, that is, electricity is our inner energy and the process unit is our brain. Now, imagine if the power is not switched on, how will the process unit work? You have an option of processing it manually, which would mean long hours of manual work, and in the end the product may not be satisfactory. The key here is to supply electricity so as to get the desired high-quality standard product.

Our human body is like this machine. In order to get the optimum benefit, we should make use of our inner energy to charge our self to achieve what we are destined to. If we switch off our inner energy or if our own energy is dormant, then we get into the loop of suffering all the time. Even when we taste success, it does not feel like being successful. With the result, we attain a very dissatisfying and unhappy life. Life is just like autumn without use of the inner energy, it seems like withering away. But if we start using our inner energy, then life tends to be like spring, blossoming with flowers, fragrance and beauty. Honestly, nobody likes to stay in the autumn of their lives, but in order to live in spring one has to shift, transform, follow and nurture the energy within to grow for us to see and reap its benefit. Think about it – no flowers really bloom without sunlight, which is also a form of energy; no trees, plants grow to their fullest without this supreme energy of sunlight. Then, why would one expects to blossom without the innate energy within one's own self?

However, it is not only the sun that plays this critical role to blossom, but it is also the soil in which the plants/ trees grow that plays a very crucial role in growth. When a seed is sowed in the soil, it embraces the seed without condition. It accepts the seed and provides all the necessary ingredients for it to grow. If there is shortage of water, the roots will either dig deep or spread wide in the soil to provide all the necessary support that a growing plant needs. But the time from when the seed is sowed till the flower and fruit it bares calls for a waiting period. The waiting period can be slightly shortened if one feeds it with the correct manure and environment.

Our brain is like the soil, which has all the components for the seed to germinate and grow. Our thoughts are seed, so when we sow a thought in our brain it starts the process of nurturing and nourishing it with the right kind of stuff needed for it to grow. However, we have to be careful about what we sow, as the output of our crop will be as per our seed type (i.e., if we sow seed of thorns, we will get thorns and if we sow seeds of flowers, we will get flowers blossoming). Similarly, if our thoughts are of fear, inferiority, undeserving and so on, the brain will process it like as is where is and give back manifold. That is, you would be more fearful, you would feel much more inferior and will have a sense of unworthiness like never before.

Similarly, if you sow the thought of being rich, happy, and prosperous, you will be presented with ample opportunities of being rich, happy and prosperous, and within no time this would have turned into reality. However, do not forget the role of the sunlight here – the inner energy that we have been talking about. The energy within us acts like the sunlight to the seed and plays a vital role in its growth. So, please do not forget to use your energy to fasten and get a better result of your thoughts.

But this is not as simple as you think it is. At times, there will be lot of conflict between the brain, the thought that you feed into your brain and your energy. Let me explain. Sometimes, you may sow the thought of becoming rich by doing a particular business which you have no interest in, but you would want to do it as you have witnessed your friend being very successful in it and you wanted to follow the suit. Now, when you sow a thought of that in your brain, the energy within you would first validate your thought. If your thoughts are accepted 100 percent by your inner energy, then you have literally hit jackpot. This means that you have found the ultimate answer and you would be heading in the right direction wherein you have the full support of your inner energy not only when required, but the external universal energy would also help you achieve your purpose 100 percent. When this actually happens, life turns into a soothing wave sound. Work has never been as pleasurable as it would be then. The time from sowing to reaping is shortened and things just unfold magically. With the blink of your eye, you have already arrived!

All this sounds very fascinating and exciting, but the trouble starts when our thoughts sowed in our brains do not resonate with our inner energy. This is when all the trouble begins and life turns out to be in turmoil and feels like you are carrying a heavy burden on yourself. This load only becomes heavier with no light at the end of the tunnel. However, people still do not get it – they just keep moving on and on endlessly. They believe that a day will come when they would get free from all these miseries. Yes, that is true, provided you change your thoughts as soon as possible and re-route your life through some inner search. Today, most of the time people are habituated to their own misery and they feel that they were born to suffer. Life for them is a struggle all the time. They are not willing to transform and they are too lazy and complacent in whatever they do. For them, doing the same thing which causes them agony and pain is far better than changing the way they think. Who can help them? It is no one but themselves. God helps those who help themselves!

And yet, there are some people who would not be satisfied with their own created misery, so much so that they would attract more negative things into their lives by sowing negative thoughts into their minds. This only reinstates their sense of being and leaves them feeling like a victim, a feeling of being a slave to this life whose reigns are held by a very few bestowed ones. If all they could have done is change their thoughts and listened to their inner self, they could have been born again as a new transformed human being. But they chose not to and condition their mind to believe that poor cannot be rich, sad cannot be happy, unsuccessful cannot be successful, unworthy cannot be worthy and so on. They ultimately become of what they think of themselves to show the world – that they were so right in their thinking and that they are so because life for them is a curse.

We are the creators of our own history and we are the drivers to change anything and everything in our lives. If one understands this simple logic, then one's life could be a pleasure and worth living every moment. During my childhood, I was forced to attend religious discourses in my school, for which I had absolutely no interest. After listening to the priest for many days, I gathered my courage to ask him, "What is it that makes our religion? And as a Zoroastrian, I also find our prayers too complicated and your discourses too vast to absorb and practice at my age." To which the priest replied, "I understand your plight, my child, and also appreciate your question. Let me answer you in very simple words. Our religion, and for that matter all the religions, teach the same thing in different words with elaborate stories, that is, good thoughts, good words and good deeds. If you just practice these three things in the true sense, you would have learnt the most important lesson of life."

I was happy with the answer, as he made my life very simple and basic. At that time, it was easy to understand, but understood the difficultly of the practicality later in life. And that brings me to another paradigm of thought: The intent behind the thought is more important than the thought alone.

Say, for example, if your thought is to become rich, but the intent could be different for different people. Some want to be rich so that they could serve the needy, while others would want to be rich so that they could pamper their ego and show off to their friends and foes, and yet others would like to dwell in the pleasures of what the riches would get them and so on. Earlier, I mentioned that when the inner energy validates the thought it also validates the intent, which is the core purpose of the energy (i.e., to guide us in the right direction). So, if the thought is validated and the intent is not, there is going to be none or anti-participation from the inner energy. One has to not only come up with a fantastic thought, but the intent behind that thought has to also resonate with the inner energy.

It is like why you want to do before what you want to do? This is because most of the time our intentions do not mirror our thoughts and actions. It is like most of the rich and famous talk about how they help the poor and call for a major press release to state how much they have given for such and such underprivileged children. Hey, now wait a minute! Was the charity done in the true sense? And if it was, then is it just another publicity stunt for positive public image? As a child, I could not distinguish between true charity and charity for publicity, so I asked my father, "What is true charity?" To which he replied, "When true charity is done with one hand, the other hand should not know about it. That is the closest you could get to true sense of charity". So true is that explanation and so simple for a child to understand. Then, why should anyone know that you have done charity? It is not going to make the person receiving it also very happy about it. Imagine, if you get something you really wanted without you knowing who has given it to you, you not only feel happy but there is also some kind of uplifting in the mystery, as against if someone has given you something and you know the person, you feel obligated and sometimes even prefer not to accept it as it does not make you feel good.

Yet, so many celebrities announce in press and various media channels that they have done charity. It is as if they are trying to hide all the darkness with the light of the deed called charity; it is like some of them hide behind their wrongdoings under the banner of charity. So guys, at times one should not get carried away by what the world is doing. Each time a wrongdoing is done, one's own energy would revolt and get back to him/her as and when the time comes. That said, one has to have clear intent of where he/she is headed with the thoughts that are to be sowed in the minds for the actions to follow.

The point to be noted here is that the intensity of the intent of the thought is directly proportionate to the realisation of the thought. This means that if your thoughts are very intense and resonates with your inner energy at deep down core level, then the realisation of the thought would be very soon. This would mean the inner energy would create havoc and get whatever it takes to get your thoughts into reality as soon as possible. It reinstates the brain again and again to work harder, in order to ensure the crop is ready to harvest before the actual time.

When there is an inner call so strong, no doubt the external universal force also comes to its rescue. But a point to be noted is that the universal energy also needs to validate your inner energy intent for which you face many different levels of difficulties. Only if you pass through the universal test of challenges will the universal energy come through to help you, and then things unfold miraculously and you would witness a moment of truth and rejoice. Sometimes, the universe puts you through the grinder for the rewards that follow are also very handsome; but some people give up midway, to only realise later that they were so close to their goals. Such are the mysterious ways of universe to test us.

Many a time, people do not understand the universal mysterious ways – it makes us realise, it makes us unlearn and then learn, it makes us exceed our limits, it makes us connect with people. Yes, it makes us connect with people. Today, we all think that the people who come into our lives are coincidences. But NO! Each and every one of them has a purpose to meet us. We attract people through universal and our own energies. Each one whom we meet has a purpose in our lives. Each one of them has something to tell us and we need to learn from each one of them.

Some of them come for a short time into our lives, while some come in for a longer time and some are with us throughout the journey. Yet, all of them are here for a purpose. They are here so we can complete the jigsaw puzzle; they are here to give us some clue to achieve our ultimate goal. All of them have a meaning in our lives and we have some in theirs; we complement each other all the time. You may now ask, "Why am I attracted to negative energies most of the time?" That also has a purpose in your life. How can you appreciate light without dark? How can you appreciate good without experiencing the bad? How can you appreciate beauty without having encountered ugly? How can you embrace success without knowing what failure is? In order to experience the positives, one has to go through some negatives. Only then there is a balance, only then one can appreciate the goodness of positivity to its completeness.

Our life is full of experiences; while some are positive and some others are negative. To test your being, the universe takes you through some experiences, wherein it is easy for you to slip into negativity. But the way you resist and evolve the temptations that the universe has to offer is the real challenge. Some sway in a different direction, while some resist the temptation and stay focused, as our subconscious brain is alert all the time. It has the ability to communicate with the universe in mysterious ways that we do not understand most of the time.

It has not been easy to pen down my thoughts, as I know the negative energy tends to throw you in the opposite direction all the time. But believe you me, to counter that, there is an innate energy that emerges from nowhere to keep me going, to keep me flowing, and the thoughts just flow, till I am completely exhausted. Such is the power of the internal and external energies.

Chapter 4

Do Not Pay Heed to Others

Yes, literally, do not give serious attention to other people's advice; not even your friends, relatives or even your parents. Let me explain you why. But before I do, let me tell you a story of a millipede and an elephant.

One morning, an elephant was lazing in the field and looking down. Suddenly, his eyes fell on a millipede that walked past him to cross the field. What really caught the elephants attention was the swiftness, grace, speed, and by the hundred pairs of legs of the millipede. He was amazed as to how this small creature was able to walk with so many legs without making any mistakes! How could he be coordinating his movement? Is he lifting the second leg after the first, followed by the fourth or the fifth? And how is it possible for him to send signals to all his 100 pairs of legs at a time? The elephant was astounded that the millipede was walking without making any mistakes and, more so, walking very fast!

The elephant constantly kept thinking about the millipede walk, so much so that he woke up the next morning and marched to the field to again observe the millipede. The millipede again appeared, walking gracefully across the field. The elephant was again amused as to how the millipede was managing his walk. What must be going on in the millipede's mind? The elephant thought, "I take so much of effort walking with my four legs, but this small creature has over hundred pairs of legs and he is walking so fast! What if he misses even one step, say his 54th leg does not move in time? This would land him in trouble! He would surely stumble and get entangled with all his 100 hundred pairs of legs!"

The more the elephant thought about the millipede, the more questions were aroused in his mind. He got restless and decided that next morning he would ask the millipede how he manages to send message to his hundred pairs of legs without making any mistakes. The next morning, the elephant again marches to the field and waits for the millipede to arrive. After waiting patiently, he sees the millipede again crossing the field. The elephant slowly approaches the millipede and stops him. He asks the millipede, "Hey, I have been observing you for many days crossing the field and I have a few questions for you." To which the millipede said, "A huge creature like you has been observing me having a walk for so many days? What is your question? Even I am eager to know." The elephant, in his enthusiasm, rattled away, "I have observed you have over 100 pairs of legs, but yet you manage to walk fast every day across the field without making a single mistake! How is that possible? What signals does your brain send to your legs? Which leg follows which leg? What if your brain commits a mistake and by mistake your 54th leg does not move in time and you could get entangled very badly?"

The millipede was amused with the elephant's questions. He thought about it for a while and then responded, "My friend, to tell you honestly, I have never thought about this, and I myself do not know how I manage to do it right all the time!" To which the elephant replied, "How is it possible? You have 100 pairs of legs and you have never thought about what if your 54th leg does not move in time, what chaos you would land into? How can you not be worried about it? It is not easy to take control of 100 pairs of legs if you miss control of even one pair! You have to think about it, as it could turn out to be very dangerous to your life!" To which the millipede responded, "Do I really need to worry about it? This kind of difficulties has never risen in my entire life!" To which the elephant responded, "May be you have a secret which you do not want to share with me." The millipede immediately responded, "No, there is no secret to this. I have no idea how I do it, but I have never bothered to think about it as each time I walk, my legs seems to know what they need to do and that to without any mistakes!" The elephant paused, "Hhmmm. I seriously would advise you to think about it as this can turn very fatal for you." Saying this, the elephant left. Now, the millipede could not help but keep thinking about what the elephant had said. The millipede thought that there must be some truth in this humongous creature's advice. He cannot be wrong! I am here with this 100 pairs of legs and what if my 54th leg does not move in time? Oh my God! That would be a disaster! The millipede now started thinking of what the elephant had told him. The more he thought about it, the more he started to believe in him, till the millipede started to believe in the elephant's advice like the gospel truth.

After that conversation, whenever the millipede started walking, he lost confidence in himself. So much so that he kept thinking about his 54th leg, and suddenly he found that his legs did not move in coordination; soon after, he stumbled and fell. The millipede thought, "All these years I was doing so well until I came across this stupid elephant, to which I paid heed and landed in this difficulty.

Next day, when the elephant met the millipede, the millipede told the elephant, "Look here, I would no more like to discuss about my walk and my hundred pairs of legs as it's none of your business". The elephant was shocked and asked as to what had happened? The millipede replied, "I have been in a mess ever since I listened to your advice. All these years I was doing well, I never had this issue of stumbling until you advised me to think about it. Now, my life has become terrible and I am fearful of each and every step I take! What have you done to me? Do you know the solution how can I get back to my original self and move on with my normal life?" The elephant replied, "Oh no, don't get me wrong! I was just trying to understand what difficulty I encounter with only two pairs of legs. You have been doing the same thing with so much of grace, elegance and effortlessly with your 100 pairs of legs. I do not have any knowledge about what you have been doing, I was just curious. I am sorry to say that I cannot help you with your current state." Saying this, the elephant hurriedly walked away and never returned to the field ever again.

In life, you will encounter a lot of people who will get amused and amazed at what you do and how you do it.

Most often, they would only raise doubts because they are full of doubts themselves. It really bothers them that how are you so successful and why they are not? They will try to give advice for which they have no knowledge about, but they just want to be a part of a conversation and attract some attention by talking about what you have been successful in. So much so that if by chance you share your future plans with them, they would not only caution you but also convince you that you would fail because they do not have any vision or knowledge what they are talking about. So, for them, the simplest route is to tell you not to do it. Their objective is to make their doubt your doubt.

One has to be intelligent and smart to NOT pay any heed to these people, as most of them do not want to do anything, and in order to be comfortable, they would like the people around them to not do anything. This is their way of being in a very comfortable zone to breed in. Just imagine, was anybody capable of telling Mr. Steve Jobs of what he was doing? Can anyone in their own true capability tell him what he was doing was right or wrong? Steve Jobs did what he had to do with full dedication and he knew all along he was doing the right thing.

We are all born with this energy within us to achieve the final purpose and we are talented, too. Most of us do not recognise our talent or our potential energy to do so. But, yet people flock in dozens to tell you that what you are doing is wrong and how difficult it is to succeed in life.

Sometime back, I watched a documentary on Mr. Amitabh Bachan, an actor and a superstar in India and one of the most sought after person for acting and dialogue delivery. A man of stature today, when just starting his career, he was rejected by the manager of a radio station for the role of a radio jockey. The manager found his voice not appropriate for the role! Today, his voice is the most sought after. What made the interviewer turn him down for the role of a radio jockey? It was beyond the manager's capacity and capability to recognise the talent sitting right in front of him.

The question here is; why should anyone believe people when they say that you cannot do the job. Have they done it or tried it? And even if they have, are they the ultimate authority to validate and approve or disapprove your capability and ability to do the work? Do they have the vision as you do? Have they been successful in what they have been doing? Do they have complete knowledge of what and how you want to do the job? If no, then why do you have to listen to them? Why do you listen to everyone around you who would tell you in many different ways how you will be unsuccessful and none will come up with one way for you to be successful?

It is a proven fact that if one keeps listening to something repeatedly for a long time, then that turns into a belief very soon. Hence, if you are surrounded by people who keep telling you how you would fail, then the seed of doubt is created in your mind. If it is allowed to grow, it then becomes your belief that you would not be able to do the job.

When Columbus declared that the earth was round, nobody believed him. They all mocked and said the earth was flat. Imagine if someone had to ask a bumblebee,

"How are you flying?" As per aerodynamics, you cannot fly due to your body weight. The bumblebee is not aware of this, and because it believes in itself to fly it has managed to fly – irrespective of physics or aerodynamics proving it wrong. The fact is that it flies in spite of the limitations. Just for a moment think that if it had known that it cannot fly, do you think if would have even made an attempt to fly?

The point I am trying to prove is that *do not believe doubts of the people around you.* Instead, listen to your inner energy and do what feels good and right. The only force that can uplift you to the desired height is your inner energy. So, trust yourself and no one else except the one (yourself) who has to decide and live your life till the end of the journey on this planet, not them!

Chapter 5

Uncover Your Gift

More than two decades ago, I visited Bangkok to see the solid gold Buddha statue weighing about 5.5 metric tonnes, about 3 meters tall and estimated to cost (at the current gold price) about US$ 300 million, aside from the artistic and intrinsic historical value, of course.

What amazed me was not the value of this magnificent idol, but the story behind this great piece of art, which I cannot resist but share. This story dates back to over 300 years ago in Thailand, wherein this magnificent gold statue belonged in a monastery. The monks in the monastery heard about the Burmese army invasion and their plan to steal all the valuables in the monastery. The monks had no intention of parting with this Buddha, something that they loved not so much for its value but for their devotion and spiritual reasons.

The monks had very little time to hide this huge statue of gold, and a challenge to hide it so that the Burmese warriors would not find it. Finally, the monks came up with a magnificent idea of covering the gold statue with a thick layer of clay knowing that the Burmese would not even touch it thinking it is worthless. The Burmese army, as predicted, invaded the monastery and took away all the valuables. However, when their eyes fell on the clay statue, they thought that it was a piece of worthless statue and did not bother to even give it a second look.

In this invasion, the Burmese warriors killed all the monks in the monastery, and thus the secret of the hidden gold Buddha remained a secret for over two centuries. In the mid-1950s, the plan to relocate the monastery was suggested, in order to make a highway at that location. The monks had to shift all the stuff from the monastery to another location, including the gold Buddha. At first, thinking that the Buddha may not be heavy they tried to lift it with help of some workers, but it turned out to be heavier than expected. They thought it would be appropriate to call for a crane to shift it.

The next day, the monks called for a crane to have it lifted, but the crane was only able to lift it over a small distance. This proved to be very time consuming, as the statue was unexpectedly heavy and additionally they had to be very careful with it as they did not want to cause any damage to the statue. It took the crane almost a full day to carry the statue to cover a small distance. To add to their woes, it started to rain heavily. So, the statue was hurriedly covered with whatever material was available in order to prevent any damage to the clay structure. Soon, it was dark and all work stopped, leaving the statue covered with various sheets available at that time.

The monks then ordered for a larger crane, which was expected to arrive the next day to transfer the statue.

Towards midnight, it started raining heavily again, so the head monk stepped out to see if the statue was adequately covered and that no damage was caused due to the rains. When the monk started to walk towards the covered statue, he was surprised to see a beam of light emitting from the statue. In the dark, he was unable to see it clearly, but he then understood that it was much more than just a clay statue. He quickly covered the statue and returned to sleep.

Next day, when a larger crane arrived to lift the statue, the head monk noticed that a crack had developed in the statue. As the sun beam hit the crack, bright light emitted from the crack in the statue. This crack only widened as the crane lifted the statue and the beam of light only became brighter and more prominent. It was then the head monk grew more suspicious and asked the statue to be lowered to the ground. Later, after inspecting the statue, he ordered the workers to break open the covered clay to unearth the real gold Buddha, whose metal body was shining like never before. Hence, the discovery of the golden Buddha that now resides in a temple in Bangkok, Thailand, is visited by millions of people every year.

We all have this bright beam of light within us, which is very powerful. However, most of us have buried it deep within us and covered with a thick layer of clay, which does not give us an opportunity to explore ourselves from within. The light here is referred to as the inner energy and the clay being false inhibitions, constant fear, complacency, negativity, laziness and so on. We are born with this wonderful gift within us, for us to discover when we grow up, but we are surrounded with people who inevitably cover our wonderful gift with a wrapper of fear, guilt, inhibitions, wrongdoing, unworthiness and so on that sometimes the gift just remains unopened!

Even if one tries to open the gift, it becomes a cumbersome process, as there are too many wrappers to be opened till we reach the actual gift of our inner light. Often, we look outside to be gifted when there is such a wonderful gift waiting to be uncovered within us. It is so close to us, yet it seems so far away! When we look at a person, sometimes we comment he/she is gifted. Yes, you are right. He/she is gifted because he/she has opened the gift. But how can you see your gift when you have not opened it yet? Some have opened their gifts and enjoying it to such an extent that others can also see the joy in which they are enveloped. But when will you open your gift?

This reminds me of a girl from a small town in India. This girl, who once struggled to find a full meal, became the winner of five world championship titles. This girl is M.C. Mary Kom, a living legend in boxing. Way back when she was practicing to pursue her dream and follow the inner light, her father, who was against her choice in career, confronted her one day asking her to make a choice between him and boxing. Mary Kom loved her father, but she knew if she had to select her father over her boxing career, she would as well be dead. She would not be able to unearth her inner gift and use her potential to reach higher, which she believed to be her real true self.

With a heavy heart, she told her father that boxing was her choice. Her father was heartbroken, but later realised what he did was unfair and that he was not allowing her to open the gift that she was born with. Finally, he realised what he did was unfair and he did apologise to her. One could not imagine what life would have been for Mary Kom if she had not brushed off the clay which was resting above her gift. The clay of poverty, the clay of orthodox father, the clay of being born as an underprivileged, the clay of being a women in a remote village and many such layers of clay that she had to brush off to release the inner light of this gift that was waiting for her to unwrap and uncover.

The gift within you is waiting to be opened. When are you going to open your gift for others to say he/she is gifted? Sometimes, people complain that they are not as gifted as others. Sometimes, their gift is out there but they are not able to see while others can see it clearly, but somehow they choose to not recognise it. This happens when you see gifts in others that you want in yourself. Sometimes, you would want the same gift that someone else has. But that is not possible. As mentioned earlier, no individual is the same. So, how can their gift be the same?

This reminds me of a friend who was born in a wealthy family. He did not know what hardship was and, as his parents were busy making money, he was left alone and hence squandered his time away.. When he was over 30 years old, he realised that people around him were busy working, while he was just splurging his family's wealth. That is when he decided that he would try to develop interest in his family business in order to portray some social standing. However, he failed – miserably. He thought that maybe he was not meant to do his family business, and then tried his hand at some other businesses. He failed miserably, again.

He finally realised that he was consistently failing and unable to figure out what he would be good at. It started affecting his health, as he was completely frustrated with his failures. Since he thought he was a cool dude, he was embarrassed when his relatives and friends questioned him as to what he was doing. He would give the safe answer – his family business. But, deep down, he knew that he was not doing the right thing. Since I was his close friend, he would ask me again and again as to what he should do. Not paying much attention to his real concern, I would suggest a business plan, which he would enthusiastically try, only to realise he had failed.

One day, he poured his heart out saying that he was miserable and that in spite of having everything he felt that he did not having anything. I then advised him to look deep into himself to unearth what he really likes and what he really enjoyed doing, to which he said that he had done this exercise many times and that there seems to be no answer to it. He told me that he gets bored with everything he does and cannot do the same thing for long. I too agreed with him, as I did not really feel he was good at anything. Although I was convinced with his inability to do anything much, I did not believe that this was the ultimate truth.

Until one day, his mother confronted me at a common friend's function where he was busy socialising with his other friends. His mother was a little drunk, and as usual was worried about her adult son wasting away his life. I was least interested in the conversation, until she told me that her son is a very kind person, to which I told myself, "Yeah, whatever!" She continued – my son always thinks of others and never about himself; one day, when my son came home without his school shoes at the age of eight she asked him, "Where are your shoes?" He innocently replied that the other boy in his school was very poor and that his shoe sole had come off and he could not afford another pair so I gave mine! His mother said that there are so many instances of his giving nature that "I do not know how he would survive in this world".

At that point, I told myself "Yes, this is it!" This is exactly the way he is going to not only survive, but live happily as well. I reached out to him and asked him if he really enjoyed giving? He nodded, and I asked him, "Don't you ever feel bored of it?" He said, "Never." I told him, "Look, I don't know whether this makes sense or not, but you seem to be a fantastic giver. You have been doing it all your life and you have been very good at it." He was stunned. He asked me to elaborate. I told him, "My friend, maybe you are here to give to this world. Not everyone can do this. You understand the needy completely and you can help them in your own little way. You have your family finances to start with and later you can have your own trust/charity/NGO firm."

Months went by, until one fine day, I happened to meet him again and he could not stop thanking me to for having shown him his purpose in life. He had already started his charity trust, wherein he was doing very well. Through word of mouth, donations had started pouring in, which only made it easier for him to concentrate on getting the right people to assist him in helping the needy. He was so happy and ecstatic about his work that he did not even feel he was working, more so when people all over praised him for his charity work. He said that this was the life he had been longing for all along and that he was happy and at peace.

The point I am trying to drive here is that we all have different and unique gifts within us and it is not necessary that we work only in one direction. Sometimes, we do not believe in the gift that we are gifted with. We see what others are doing and question our own inner self. The question is, "Why do we constantly compare ourselves with others, when we are completely different from others?" Our individual purpose is different from others, but we all work towards the same bigger purpose. We all have our parts to play. The question here is, "Do we earnestly play our role or are we mimicking others all the time?"

Chapter 6

Why Me?

My whole life, I have heard many people complaining about why me? Why did I get cancer? Why did I lose my job? Why have I gone bankrupt? Why did my dear one meet with an accident? Why am I unsuccessful? Why am I not wealthy? Why am I weak? Why do I have to take all the responsibilities? Why does this happen to me all the time? Why me? Why me? Why me?

Does this, by any chance, resonate with you? If yes, then read on. Soon, you are going to eliminate the "why me", from your life. We human beings unknowingly invite most of the unpleasant events in our lives. And when bad things happen to us, we still do not comprehend that and invite more such events into our lives.

First, let us talk about one of the deadliest disease on earth – cancer. Till now, science has not found a 100 percent cure for it. But, yet some survive and others do not. The estimate is that 9 million people are going to suffer from cancer in 2015, but we will witness that most will escape from having cancer. So, what really causes cancer?

If you ask any doctor, I bet you will have differences of opinion. With all due respect, nowadays, most doctors try to treat the disease, but rarely will a doctor invest in treating the patient. I believe that one has to treat his/her own self to avoid such diseases. Human beings are prone to get any and all types of diseases, it is up to him/her to prevent it or attract it. Yes, I repeat it is up to him/her to prevent or attract any diseases.

When I say attract, it could be through physical, mental or inner gut feelings. Let us now get into specifics to get a clear understanding of it. When I say physical, I mean what we eat, drink, and breathe or inject ourselves with. If we continue to eat junk and unhealthy food all the time, we are bound to contract some deadly diseases. Remember, when I spoke about eating meat, how unhealthy it is for our inner energy – not only that it is very bad for our body if eaten in big quantities, but it is also very unhealthy for our inner energy. Drinking alcohol in large quantity, smoking and intake of abusive substances are all very harmful for us, but we still do not pay much heed to what we get into our system, so long as it gives us temporary feel-good factor. However, most of us are aware that when it comes to eating food, what is good and what is not as taught to us from our childhood (hopefully it is the right information). Unfortunately, our education system does not pay much emphasis on what we think.

If we fear something time and again, one fine day it would be right in front of you. There have been instances when people who just by their negative thinking attracted deadly diseases. Yet, there are some who have been completely cured of a deadly disease by positive affirmation. It is ones pure belief system that plays a vital role in attracting/avoiding diseases. Now, you many tell me that by that logic everyone in this world would be free of all diseases. Yes, you are right. But ask yourself a simple question: how many of us have a strong belief system? When one thought comes in to our mind, then immediately another thought rejects it! However, when another thought comes in, the other thought shows its way out! This just goes on, and we have no one but the poor doctor who only tries to treat the disease and not you. The result is that you get the disease again! And, if you are lucky, the doctor would save you again, but how long can he save you from that disease?

In most cases, where I have witnessed deadly diseases like cancer, which has happened to people having healthy eating habits, is due to some deep unhappiness, sorrow, fear, not wanting to live, depression and so on. These feelings directly impact our inner energy level, and if these feelings manifest for long in our body, it would then convince our inner energy to attract something deadly that would bring an end to our lives. Let me tell you what one of my close friends has been going through, in order to make you understand what I mean.

A close friend of mine had been living with her mother for several years. She was not keen on getting married as she felt that her mother would be left alone and neglected. She sacrificed her life and continued to stay with her mother, who was getting old. After a few years, her mother passed away. As my friend was not able to accept her death, she went into depression. She had lost her dear mother, who had been with her all the time. Her love for her mother was very strong and that she could just not come to terms with the fact that she was no more. Days, weeks and months went by, and she still was unable to come out of her depression. No amount of counselling would get her back to her old self. She would constantly ask the almighty that what happened to her was not fair and that she had no wish to live anymore on this earth.

Her condition did not improve even after a year. All she would do is curse herself for being alive and that she had lost the purpose of her living. One day, she developed a severe pain in her chest. The pain only intensified with time. She was forced to see a doctor by one of her well-wishers. The doctor told her that she had to undergo a series of test, which was done the following day. When the reports came in, she was diagnosed with breast cancer!

She was shocked and got extremely depressed about it. She got weaker by the day. Although she was undergoing treatment for the cancer, she showed no signs of improvement and had soon reached stage 3 of cancer. Then, one fine day, she had a heart-to-heart talk with her sister, who made her understand that she should have a will to live. She had to change her attitude towards life in order to change her body condition. Only if she came to terms with her mother's death and the will to live a life with happiness, only then the treatment would work on her. Somehow, her sister's talk worked. For the first time, I saw in her eyes that she wanted to live and not die! She became very positive, and guess what? Her medical reports showed positive progress for the first time. Her cancerous growth had stopped and was reducing day by day. She was on her way to getting cured of cancer!

What really changed in her life? Why did she get cancer in the first place? It was all her own doing. She called upon this deadly disease, and then she herself asked it to go. When she did not have the will to live, all the energy units in her system were attuned to what she really wanted. Until then, there was a major shift wherein she invoked her inner energy to do otherwise, and rightly the inner energy had been working hard towards it. This is just one of the cases I have witnessed. There are many more similar instances that I have come across. The key is our belief and using our energy to attract or distract energy within and outside us against these deadly diseases. But, change is needed and is a must. Depending on the cause that triggered the disease, it has to be reversed. In my friend's case, she had called upon the disease, and hence she had to let go of it in the same way.

Similarly, most of us attract incidents in our lives by just thinking about it and aligning our inner energy for it to come true. However, most of the time we are not aware that it will happen; all we do is be afraid about some dangerous situations that may occur in our lives. I have witnessed it in many of my colleagues and friends. One instance which is still fresh in my mind is about my distant relative who has two sons. All she would do constantly is worry about her sons. She would read in the newspaper about some accident or watch some news on television of some incident, and later she would visualise the same happening to her sons.

Whenever I met her, she would narrate her plight, to which I told her to stop it immediately and that there was no need to worry and all would be well for her and her sons. She did not listen to me and kept worrying praying that her sons should be safe and not meet with any accidents. In a short while she heard about an accident of a boy who resided next to her building. She was petrified and called to tell me how accidents are frequent in her area and what if it happens to her children. I once again warned her to not think in that direction, to which she responded, "I can't help but think about these things". After a few days, I received a call from her that her son had met with a serious accident!

However, some may call it a coincidence. But I will not. I had warned her time and again that the same would happen to her sons, as she was only calling for it day in and out. For her, it was just a fearful thought, but in reality there was a whole universal energy working towards her thought and fear to come true. Most people fear the unknown. All they constantly think is, "What if this happens or what if that happens?" And it is but natural that these thoughts, if not stopped, would snowball into reality. So, the best thing to do is to deal with it by negating it in the beginning and keep evading it whenever it creeps into our minds and later into our inner energy system. If we make it a habit to negate it constantly and think positively, we will automatically be tuned to attracting positive things into our lives.

However, this may be easy for some to practice, for some to achieve it with difficulty and yet some would reach there with lots of persistence and practice. But for some it may be extremely difficult and not achievable no matter how much they try. In that case, I would suggest a personal life coach to help them achieve the desired result. This process may be a little slow, but the result has tremendous benefits for life.

Some of you, who are reading this book, may like to ask me as to what if you have already attracted deadly diseases or met with an accident? What should you do? I would say, "Accept the present gracefully, think positive all the time, and then move all the positive energy within and externally to help you achieve the desired result". Remember, miracles do happen when doctors give up hope. You can turn around the situation and make things work in your favour. The universal energy is kind and is in abundance. All you need to do is reach out. "Ask and you shall receive". We all know this, but yet some of us ask/think about things we do not want in our lives. All we need to do is profess for things we want in our lives, like good health, peace, love, surrounded with caring and kind people and so on. Do, what you were born to do and be successful, be happy!

So simple, yet so complicated for most to understand and follow. I was born into a family of eight. My father did very well for himself, until the government took over his land and property under the road-building act, leaving him with no compensation. Since he was educated, he was able to shift gears from a restaurant owner to a working professional. However, at times it was difficult to make ends meet. At that tender age, I would profess to be very well off with multiple properties and cars to travel in. I distinctively remember that I wanted to reside in a tower building and believed in it 100 percent. Somehow I had the feeling that it was going to be true in the near future. When I shared my thoughts with my family, they would mock me and told me to stop living in a dream world and face reality. I never paid any heed to them. The inner voice was so strong that I would turn around and say, "It's just the matter of time. I am going to get there". They thought that I was too young to be taken seriously. Even at that tender age, I knew I was going to be successful in achieving my financial goal and that nothing in this world would deter me from it.

Those days, I did not know how I would achieve my goal, but I knew that I would make it. The energy within me was restless all the time. It had received a strong dictate to achieve my financial goal from a very early age. I knew it and I was sure. What I was upset about was that no one believed me, in spite of telling them several times. I continued my journey without the slightest of doubt, and here I am living in a tower building with a few cars at my disposal and a chauffeur to drive me around, and yes, a weekend get-away home. I made it by beating all odds, but I strongly believed in myself and my inner energy to work towards my goal. And, to make it all worthwhile, I knew all along that I was going to make it, and I did no matter what people around told me!

This invoking of the inner energy somehow works for me all the time. Be it a small or a mammoth task like achieving financial independence from having nothing. So, let me narrate some small incidences from my school days. I was an average student, but somehow secured first position in drawing, art, acting and elocution. And, to me, not so surprising was once securing first position in sports, which was to my knowledge unachievable if I had only practiced and not believed in me. I was good at studies, naturally inclined towards art and acting, but extremely poor in sports. So, when the annual sports day would arrive, I would make a good spectator cheering with the crowd. Till, one fine day, I decided that though I did not have interest in sports I wanted to secure first position just for one time. I wanted to challenge myself and wanted to know how my inner energy would support me to achieve my desire to win in sports, which was my weak spot.

What I did was I studied all types of sports and my inner energy prompted me to put in less effort into practice and training to gain the desired results. My interest was captured by the long jump. I thought that this sport was where I did not have to put in months of practice, the way I would have probably done for running. I knew my competitor's highest scores for the last few years. No one knew that I was secretly preparing for the long jump, and my aim was to beat the last few years' highest score with a decent margin. As days went by, I practiced with a vengeance and affirming to my inner energy that I need to win this event at any cost. When I ran for the long jump during my practice, my inner voice would resonate telling me yes, you can do it. I saw my scores improving with each day of the practice.

The final sports day arrived, and my opponent was shocked to see me on the field. She had a mocking smile on her face, which said that I was no competition to her. To which my inner energy responded, "Let the scores speak for it". My opponent had her jump before me, and then it was my turn. I told myself this is it. I have to win, as now it was the question of my prestige. My energy was very positive and I ran like never before, with full force and energy. There was not a single moment wherein I doubted my capability and ability to win. And guess what? I won the long jump event, securing the first position in that category. The moment was filled with joy, and I understood then that when one invokes the inner energy it would never let you down.

The point I am trying to make here is that it is not about winning, it is about how one wins. The key is to trigger the inner energy force to achieve your desired goal. The instances kept recurring in my life, from childhood till date. Another instance was about me participating in a fancy dress competition. As we all know, fancy dress competition is about how well you dress and also on how well one enacts the character he/she is playing. When I participated, I knew that I could not afford a fancy dress, but I also wanted to desperately win the competition. So, after some thinking, I decided to become a mad beggar as all it needed was some torn clothes which we had in abundance. I was certain that I would not win the competition if my act was not outstanding, as only dressing as a mad beggar was not an effort at all.

So, my quest was to enact the role so well that I would be the undisputed winner. I took help of my elder brother and we scripted a hilarious and entertaining anecdote. I practiced in front of whoever was available at home and urged them for an opinion, wherein I could better the script and act. The night before the competition, I could not sleep; I was restless. I kept repeating that I had to win the competition as this would only affirm my faith in me and my energy within.

The day of the competition had arrived, and when I observed my competitors, it sent shivers down my spine. But there was an inner voice telling me that my act would supersede all. It did not matter how well the others were dressed or how poorly I was dressed. My act on the stage would be the game changer. When my name was announced, I told myself, "This is it!" For a few seconds, I was in a hypnotic state and I felt as if some energy within me took over. The force and energy helped me deliver the dialogue. I could hear only laughter all over. I had to pause for a few seconds to calm the audience down and continued with the dialogue. My confidence increased as the audience continued laughing at my dialogue. After the competition, guess what? I was announced the winner!

We all have this energy within us, but very few use it. Some of us use it without being conscious about it, like I did during in my childhood. Yet, most of us are oblivious to it. The key is to attune into ourselves with the energy within and trigger it time and again to make it work in our favour – to achieve our desires with very little challenges. People who are aware of it and practice it have been reaping tremendous benefits from it. It just takes time to consciously experience its power to reckon with it, and then reap the rewards. My earnest attempt here is to make you experience this power just once. That is good enough for you to help you discover the journey thereafter. So guys, what are we waiting for? At least make an attempt!

Chapter 7

Signs to Look Out For

Even though we are not successful in tapping our inner energy, our inner energy constantly makes an attempt to guide us and help us. Like it not only helps us carry out a mammoth task of finding out our purpose in life, it also guides us in our trivial or sometimes daily activities. This way, it makes us feel its presence, and it is up to us to recognise its presence. It is like a small baby who cries to draw our attention. Similarly, the inner energy communicates with us by showing us some signs to lead us in the right direction. Most people are oblivious or simply ignore it.

The danger of ignoring it for a long time may suppress the energy within us. It is like a baby crying for a long time to grab your attention, but if you ignore it for long, the baby would get exhausted and go to sleep. Similarly, if one does not listen to the inner voice for a long time, the voice would eventually fizzle off and remain silent/dormant. But, on the other hand, if one pays heed to it and harness the skill to follow the signs, it would eventually turn out to be beneficial for you. The inner energy knows what is good for you and would always point you in the desired direction, provided you have harnessed the positive energy within you.

Let me give some examples while still fresh in my mind. When I travelled to the United Kingdom with my husband, I was unaware that I had already conceived a baby. Since we visited most of our friends, we partied almost every other day; liquor, at times, was unavoidable. To my surprise, I continued seeing many pregnant ladies. At first, I thought I was becoming a little crazy. But later, while waiting outside a theater, I discussed this phenomenon with my husband. I told him that nowadays I was noticing lots of pregnant women. He said, "Really? I have not seen any!" As soon as he finished talking, two pregnant women passed us by. Both of us looked at each other with amusement. From then on, we started seeing pregnant women everywhere. We also jokingly discussed what if I was pregnant, to which we did not pay much heed to.

After reaching home a few weeks later, it was confirmed that I was pregnant! I was then able to relate as to why I saw so many pregnant ladies who caught my attention. It was a sign, for which I never caught on. I was so close, yet so oblivious. The sign was there to protect me. It was telling to take care of myself as I was pregnant. Now that I think back, how better it could have unfolded than showing me so many pregnant women. I was not able to pick the sign and connect it to my pregnancy. So, in life, there are many signs which protects, guides, directs us, but it is our unconscious mind that is unable to pick it up in time.

Another sign, which I picked up, was during the school admission of my daughter. We scouted around for good schools in our town; however, most did not appeal to us. We were just not happy with the schools we visited, and over a period of time it became extremely difficult to take decision. The admission closure date was fast approaching, and we had yet to decide on a school. I distinctly remember the time on a flight while flipping through a magazine my eyes fell on an article about a school which had all the facilities, including some impressive achievements. I thought that I would definitely check this school out after returning home. However, I completely forgot about the school and continued with my daily work. One day, while returning home from work, my eyes fell on a billboard – it was an advertisement for the school I had read about. Now, call it coincidence or good advertising, I happened to see it. But I still did not inquire about the school.

The following day, while talking to my friend about my daughter's admission, she promptly recommended the school which I had read and seen all along. I decided that this school deserved a visit. This turned to be, so far, the best school (according to me). The next day, my husband and I went to see the principle of the school. We both were very happy with the school, and promptly got our daughter admission into the school. No sooner had we done this, the school was declared the best school in town; also, I never cease to be amazed with my daughter's progress.

What amuses me about signs is that it appears one after the other in series like a sequence. One may shrug off saying its mere coincidence, but to me these are signs. Just like when I was flipping through the flight magazine with little interest (I never go through them when I am traveling), but somehow I picked it up, browsed through it and this school advertisement caught my attention. I am sure there may have been several other schools that must have advertised, but my attention was drawn to this one. Similarly, there are so many billboards. Why did this particular one catch my attention? And soon after, my friend recommending this school was also amazing. The voice within us makes several attempts to guide us when we need help or when we are in danger. Its sole purpose is to guide us in the right direction. It is up to us to follow the voice or ignore it.

The interesting part about writing this book is that I first looked deep into my inner self to see if I am on the right path or not. To find this, I meditated and communicated with my inner self and asked that if I am on the right path, I do need to see some signs in the next few days; only then would I go ahead with the project. Next day, my uncle mentioned an author who had received an award for writing a few good books. The same day, I heard some friends discussing about a book. I lost interest in the conversation. But the only word which resonated in my ears was book, book and book! I thought, maybe, this is just a coincidence. Later, while talking to another friend, she also started talking about some book.

Again, when I opened a newspaper, my attention was drawn to an article about a bestseller in New York. That evening, when I switched on the television, the first thing I hear is a controversy about some book. I was stunned, for what I had called for was right there in front of me. I could feel the inner voice asking me, "Do you need any more validations?" For few minutes, I was scared. I had never experienced this before and I somehow felt apologetic for having done that. But I am certain about one thing now – I made a promise to myself that I will have this book completed and published! And here is the book!

Sometimes, I feel that for many of us life is like sipping a cup of coffee, with each sip so bitter as one can feel the absence of sugar. Even though the coffee is bitter, one cannot do without it due to being addicted to it. After having sipped almost till the bottom of the cup, you discover that the sugar has settled there. All you needed was to stir it with a spoon to enjoy a lovely cup of coffee. However, it too late as the coffee is over. Similarly, in life, all we need to do is look within and bring out our inner energy to have a very interesting and enjoyable life. But most of us are oblivious to our inner energy, just like the sugar in a coffee cup. One goes through pain and suffering till the end, only to discover that what you did was not what you were meant for. But by then, it is too late as you have reached the end of your life.

However, the end of life is not the end of our energy's journey. Our energy moves on and resides in another form. However, transition from one form to another may take a little longer, but it is certain. One has to come back to earth sooner or later to accomplish the ultimate goal. Now, let us talk about karma, which seems to be so complex, but yet so simple.

Chapter 8

Karma

Karma has been described by many religions in their own way. People mostly think that because of their karma they will encounter a definite destiny. To which, according to me, is not true. Karma is about doing some action or even a thought. Each action or thought will trigger a reaction. So, depending on what we do, there is a reaction.

So, if the action we perform is bad, we will get a bad reaction and if our action is good, we will get a good reaction. However, the time of reaction as to when it will occur is not definite, but that it will happen is certain. Also, the magnitude of reaction is mainly based on the intent of the action and not the action itself. Let me explain what I mean by that.

When one does a good deed, of say helping the poor with the intent of bettering their lives out of love and helping nature, it definitely is good karma. But if charity is done to look good in the eyes of the media and gain good publicity, it is bad karma. Although the action is good and the amount of charity given is also very high, the intent is not good. It automatically turns to bad karma and one will attract a bad reaction to it.

The reaction to a bad or a good karma is not instantaneous. Sometimes, it may take few seconds, while sometimes it may take a few hours, days, months, years, a lifetime or sometimes it could be carried on to another life. What I have noticed and experienced with people around me and myself is that most of the time the reaction is manifold. Maybe the action is accumulated to give back a compounded return. Also, if one expects some good to happen out of the good deed you perform, it never really happens. It nullifies the good deed because there is intent of wanting a good karma to return.

My elders always told me to do a good deed, forget about it and never ever expect any good to happen in return. This way, the good karma gets accumulated and comes to you at the right time, which is so amazing that you wonder why these good things are happening to you while the world around you is suffering.

For example, you see a colleague continuously doing wrong things but not suffering and happily prospering without any kickbacks from its bad karma. But, as mentioned earlier, the return is not immediate. In most cases, it takes much longer than expected. However, when karma strikes back, it is a real big one. It snow balls as time passes with greater momentum and vengeance, so much so that it completely breaks the person, making it very difficult to revive.

So, when one sees a good person suffering, it may not be his current karma that he is paying for; it is the past life karma that has been carried forward and he has to go through what he has signed up for. Each one is born differently and has to go through the suffering of karma even if one has not done anything wrong in this life. Even thinking about a bad deed would result into a bad karma, and the only reason for most people that life is a big curse and suffering.

But do remember that to lead a happy and prosperous life is in one's own hands. Also, one cannot blame karma for the entire life, as building on positive karma is in one's own hands; and we have the ability to change our bad karma balance to a good karma balance. It is like, for example, when you are in debt you have to pay the interest, and when you start to save and pay up your principle amount borrowed, you not only stop paying interest but you also would gain interest from the savings!

Such is the principle of karma. So, ensure that you continuously do good deeds without expecting any returns. Good deeds are not only measured monetarily, but also measured in action, intent, feelings, physical touch, words and so on. So, your action and inaction both would cause bad or good karma. For example, you witness a crime is being committed and you choose to turn a blind eye to it. You feel that since you were not involved in the crime, you have not committed any bad karma. Wrong! Since you looked the other way and not help prevent the crime or report it, you have committed a wrong by not taking any action. Hence, you have to face a bad karma because of your inaction towards the crime.

If you tell me that in spite of the fact you have never caused harm to others, you are still unhappy, my questions to you would be: "Have you monitored your thoughts? Are they positive most of the time?" Because any negative thought would also snowball into bad karma. Thinking evil or being jealous of someone is good enough to gather bad karma, as it pollutes our inner energy to become negative and, in turn, it attracts a similar energy which would only make you suffer or lead a miserable life.

Although you may do lots of good deeds anticipating good returns, it may backfire on you; and you may end up gathering bad karma for your actions, which are not pious and pure. Or sometimes it is just your previous karma that you have to pay for in this life. Relax! Just do good things in life; go with what feels right and not with what is right. Sometimes lying could save someone's life, for telling the truth may take away that someone's life. Keep in mind that in life, everything is relative and nothing is in isolation.

There is an old saying: "What goes around; comes around". This is so true, because everything must come to an end, with the source being the start point and the end point. The circle of karma must be completed. This reminds me of a story of an emperor.

There was once an emperor, who was very proud of himself and did not believe in karma. One day, he thought that since he was the ultimate power in his town he could get away with anything. One day, he called his minister and slapped him in front of all the people present. With a loud laugh, he said, "I know I can never take this back". So saying, the emperor walked away. The minister was shocked and was in no position to question the king. After thinking about the incident, he called his subordinate and he too slapped him hard and said, "This is a game king has started, so you carry forward the game by slapping another person. Tell that person that the slap must be passed on and whoever would not obey would be punished".

The subordinate got worried, as he was in no position to not obey his king. So, to carry the game forward, he slapped his colleague and passed on the message. The slapping continued all over the town throughout the day. When the king was getting ready for bed, the queen told him that she needed to complete a task before she, too, could retire. The king surprisingly asked, "What is the task?" The queen answered that she would only answer if he would not get angry at her. The king promised the queen that he would not get mad, and so the queen slapped the king! The king was surprised and asked her the reason why. The queen replied, "It seems you had started it and the whole town has been slapped, until my mother slapped me and told me to slap you to put an end to this."

Finally, the king understood that no matter who you are, you cannot be oblivious to karma, and that what goes around comes around sooner or later! Hence, do not challenge karma, as it will be there when you least expect it.

If same thing happens to you again and again, you wonder why? For example, someone getting betrayed time and again by his close friends; or someone's promotion withheld time and again due to some politics in the organization; or your partner happens to cheat on you all the time and so on. These instances keep repeating in our lives till we find a reason for it. One has to learn from it and deal with it in the right way. It is a learning process wherein the instances keep repeating endless number of times in your life. If one deals with the situation in the same way and has not learnt from it, the instance would keep repeating like a never-ending loop. Or sometimes it is just the past karma that comes back to you in manifold.

The key is not to get upset or angry, but to be conscious about karma. Never try to harm anyone, even if that someone has been bad to you, as this would only add on to your bad karma. You need to concentrate on your work and let karma take its own course to get back at your foes.

World is governed by laws; however, everything in life is subjective. According to me, intent is the most critical part of any action. There is no right or wrong. But one has to bear the consequences of one's actions. So, if a person is ready to bear the consequences of harming someone, it is his prerogative. Again, I would like to reiterate that one should have the right intent behind every action he/she takes. One can escape the law of land, but one cannot escape the law of karma. It will haunt you and get back to you when the time is right.

One has to strive and continuously built positive karmas, as it would only help them achieve their goals faster without many hindrances. Do not worry, or even try to get back at people who have done you harm, if your karma is good there will be a time wherein you will get an opportunity to sit back and look at them when the karma strikes them. You can have a good laugh then; so, why waste your energy of getting back to your foes and increase your bad karma?

With this topic at an end, we will now discuss about focusing and visualising positivity.

Chapter 9

Visualise Positivity

Our actions are creation of our thoughts, and hence it is extremely important what we think. Though I have briefly touched upon this topic earlier, I would like to dwell on this topic a little more, as the root of all the problems and solutions is our thoughts. It may sound ridiculous, but what I strongly believe and have witnessed is even if we think bad about someone, the bad karma increases and we get hit by it hard when least expected. So is the reverse mechanism – if we think well about someone, we automatically increase our good karma and we start to experience positive occurrences.

How does it work would be your question to me. When we think of something, we visualise it in our minds; we tend to form a picture of an action or a doing. This sends signals to our inner energy, which then starts to act upon it. It gathers all the force from within and sometimes from outside to make it real, if within its capacity and capability. What is interesting is the energy within us is programmed to work for us. So, if we think of a bad doing for others, the energy within us also starts to manifest to make the action possible for ourselves. What it tries to do is match the picture visualised by us into reality.

For example, a friend of mine wanted to get married for a long time, but was not able to meet the right man. She was looking for a man who would be caring, well to do, good looking, with healthy habits and compatible with her. To my knowledge, these are a few reasonable wants from any average eligible spinster. One day, during dinner, she told me how frustrated she was as she was yet single and attracting guys who were either smokers, or an alcoholic, or not good looking and so on. I decided to find out more, and so asked her, "What do you really think about?" She replied, "I told you what kind of person I want, right? So, that's what I also think!" I reiterated, "Can you please be explicit and tell me what exactly you think?"

To which she replied, "Oh, okay. If you insist, I just tell myself I don't what a smoker, an alcoholic, a person who doesn't care, who is not ugly". Now I understood her plight of meeting all the people she wanted to avoid but would visualise just the opposite, and that is exactly what she attracted. When she visualised that she did not want a person who smoked, she was actually visualising a person smoking. The result was that her inner energy was geared to attract a smoker and present it to her! Similarly, she attracted all the other people by strongly visualising them, and they were attracted to her as she thought about them day in and out.

I advised her to stop doing that, due to which she has been attracting all the wrong people in her life as she has been visualising them. I advised her to visualise a positive good-looking person and not think of any smoke or drinks along with it. She did not believe me at first, but promised that she would try. And guess what? It worked! She started attracting all the right men into her life, until she settled with one and is happily married today!

The point I am trying to drive here is that one has to think positive. Continuous positive thinking can convert the negative energy into positive. Most of us are born with a neutral energy within us. The energy is pure and in its nascent stage. It is then exposed to everything around. The influence of mind is tremendous on the energy within, and at the nascent stage it can be easily altered. One has no control over what a little child thinks when exposed to this world.

The energy level and type is developed in the mother's womb. It is a belief that expecting mothers must not see or hear any violence as it impacts a child brain. To my thinking, it is the energy type and levels that get influenced if the expecting mother constantly sees or hears violence.

Many successful people, when asked what they do, give the inevitable answer "I am a dreamer". In literal sense, when one constantly dreams of good things happening, in reality it does happen. And, if coupled with hard work, the dream becomes reality even faster. As a child, I visualised an apartment that I currently reside in. I did that not because I was aware of this technique, but because it felt good, even if it meant a momentary pleasure of just dreaming of being in the type of apartment I wanted to be in. So much so that I literally believed in my dreams without any doubt that today, when I look back, I understand so well.

When I visualise, I do it with great intensity and details. I do it as if I am already there and that the future that has to come is the one I am living in. I can feel the breeze, smell fresh air, feel the sunlight piercing my skin, a positive bout of energy urging me to get going and so on. I also visualised my friend and relatives with me in that very moment. I pay attention to every detail, such as the expression on their faces and so on. I pay attention to their expressive eyes, smile, voice, body language and also their emotions and the touch.

I also make note of the furniture and fixtures that surrounds us. I observe how each item is placed neatly; I note how each piece of furniture and art has been placed aesthetically; I enjoy the color and design of the furniture; I appreciate the art work framed on the walls with perfect reflection of lights; I notice the vibrant color of the wall paint and the shine on the Italian marble floorings.

I visualise a very happy gathering, with cocktails and drinks being served; I visualise that there is going to be many more occasions of success being celebrated in a classy and elegant way. The list of visualisation can be endless. This is just to give you a preview of visualisation. The more details and specific one visualises, the more certainty of realisation is witnessed. The frequency and intensity of visualisation is also of paramount importance.

To make it easier for first timers, it is advisable to visualise early in the morning or just before going to bed at night. To my experience, these timings have been the most favourable, as there is less distraction and the time to channelise our energy is also perfect. In the morning, the mind is fresh and ready to take on new tasks. The time when one is just about to sleep is also ideal, as the mind and body has already performed the daily task and is now ready to relax. In this state, whatever is fed into our minds stays for a longer time in the subconscious mind, which then connects with the inner energy at a sublime level.

However, one can experiment with one's own self to see what works best and stick to the comfort level of the timing preferred. Most come back to me saying that they have been meditating and visualising every day for hours, only to discover that the things are just not unfolding as per their wishes. To this, I asked one of my friends, "How long do you visualise?" She answered, "About 30 minutes morning and evening." I further inquired, "What do you visualise?" She responded, "I visualise becoming a successful entrepreneur". "So, what are your thoughts about it throughout the day?" I asked. She replied, "I constantly worry about; how am I going to achieve my goals, as I have loads of restrictions to achieve it".

There you go! How can you expect to visualise for an hour which is positive and then visualise for the rest of the day about all the fears within you? Consciously or subconsciously, you are preparing a platform for you to fail! This is going against the basic principle of visualisation. A negative thought process throughout the day would outshine an hour of positive visualisation. The fear factor destroys the belief system which one tries to develop via visualisation. It is like eating one healthy meal a day followed by eating junk food the rest of the day, and one expects to be in perfect health which is next to impossible.

Similarly, visualisation for few minutes a day will not help. One has to believe in the thoughts and positively think about it day in and out. More the positive reinforcement the closer the thoughts would reach its reality. If one puts in a good amount of hard work with positive thinking and visualisation, then the achievement of the desired result is inevitable. One has to be focused all the time and not deviate from the goals to be achieved. Sometimes, one is close to the goal, but a slight distraction or negative thinking can make us feel the goal unachievable.

The key is to avoid all the negative distraction. As we use the power of our inner energy with lot of positivity, we are also disrupting the overall energy balance around us. Hence, we encounter some negative experience caused to slow our pace to maintain the energy balance. One has to continuously work in the positive direction without any disbelief to achieve ones goals. All successful people have gone through series of challenges, but they have all fought negativity to emerge as winners.

So, what are you waiting for? Go ahead and visualise and battle the way up to glory of victory, pride, honor and happiness!

Chapter 10

Beware of the Rub-Off Effect

When I say rub-off effect, I mean the effect which other energies have on yours. Let us consider a person with loads of negative energy comes in contact with you and will influence you and your energy to a large extent. There is a possibility that his/her energy would flow into you and you may get affected by the negative energy.

This energy will not only pollute your inner energy, but it will also pollute the environment. The presence of the energy is quite prominent and is felt by one even after the person has left. One has to be conscious about this energy and must try to neutralise it as far as possible. When I say neutralise I mean to nullify the energy.

One of the best ways to neutralise the energy is to mop the house with salt water; also, one can bathe with salt water to rub off the negative energy; open the doors and windows to allow more ventilation; try to keep fans at high speed for some time; try to dust the furniture and fixtures in your house daily; try to circulate fresh air into your house to replace any bad or negative energy residing in your house brought in by any negative person.

Most people do not understand or feel the energy of other people. For starters, try to wear someone else's jacket, which has been worn by the owner for a long time. When you put on the jacket for the first time, you will feel a little uncomfortable, but as time passes the uncomfortable level would most likely lessen. This is because some of the owner's energy has settled in the jacket. Some of this energy would transfer to another person who would wear the jacket. Hence, the uncomfortable feeling! Though it is not necessary that the energy may transfer to the person who would wear the jacket, it does happen in some cases.

Have we not heard about the clothes of celebrities or a very successful person being auctioned at exorbitant prices? For example, a gown of the late Princess Diana sold for US$ 1.2 million, Madonna's clothes were auctioned at US$ 3.2 million, while the late Michael Jackson's items fetched over US$ 5 million! Now, just pause for a moment and think. Why would people spend so much to acquire clothes worn by famous people? Does it not sound obnoxious? People are willing to pay a fortune to buy used clothes? Now, why is that?

The underlying belief is to get a small fraction of these famous personalities' energy into their home. They just wish that some of this energy would have a rub-off effect on them. The belief is that even if the person has passed away, the energy within their clothes is still alive. People are enamored with the celebrities and willing to pay a fortune for a small portion of their energy, which may have been trapped in some of their items, clothes or accessories. The reason for purchasing celebrity clothes could be something else, but there is definitely more to it than just a used dress.

My attempt here is to make you aware and conscious about the energy, which is found all around us and to stay away from unwanted, bad or negative energies. The reflection of the inner energy is not only confined within our body, but it also emits outside our body. This energy that envelope the entire body is termed by most people as aura. Aura is nothing but the projection of our inner energy.

A very light and bright aura is pure and positive energy, while a dull and darker aura enveloping the body usually is negative aura. So, if one is conscious about the aura, one would be able to see negative and positive energies right through. There have been books on various colours of aura, but to my belief that is incorrect. There are no aura colors. It is just a bright light, which varies in intensity and brightness. Sometimes, I miss the aura, but I can definitely feel the energy of an individual.

I can not only feel the energy of an individual, but I can also sense it, if the individual is concealing some facts or transparent about his/her dealings. I can see it if the intent of the person is not clear. I can also sense if the person is internally not well. Surprisingly, sometimes I can even sense what goes on in his/her mind. You may think that I am not telling you the truth, but just think – has it not happened to you when you said something while the other person tells you that I was also thinking about the same thing. It is not necessary that you both to be at the same place. You could be miles apart.

This happens because the energy within us has the power to communicate even without any verbal or nonverbal communication. It is like minds talking to minds; it is like our energies talking to each other. However, to experience this, one has to be connected to the other person. And also, if you wish to know the other person's thoughts, you have to really focus and concentrate. It is scary, right? This is because science has not yet proved it. It is being practiced only in certain areas without any research or proof. Only the person experiencing it can understand, and many are oblivious to it.

For example, when you are in love, only you know what is going on. You cannot express it or make the other person feel the way you feel. You can only cherish and enjoy its beauty and only you can experience its pain.

At times, you may have come across people passing a comment about you – you sound/act like your friend/ relative/ acquaintance. Now, why is that? This is because you have been spending too much time with that person and there has been some rub-off effect on you. Spending more time with a person would mean that you will acquire some behavioral traits of that person. You may start thinking, to some extent, the way he/she thinks. Your personality also gets influenced by him/her. Similarly, your energy also gets affected by his/her energy.

However, behavior, personality can be taken care of easily, but if the inner energy has been affected negatively it would take a long time for cleansing. Hence, one has to be wary of whom one interacts and spends time with, as it would turn out to be beneficial to you as well as harmful.

Practice listening to your inner voice. If the inner voice tells you to interact more with others, then please go ahead and do so. If you inner voice tells you move away, then I suggest you maintain a distance. Always go with the decision the inner voice tells you, as it can never be wrong. However, listening to your inner voice needs practice, perseverance and meditation. Every one cannot listen to their inner voice. To some, it comes naturally, to some with practice, and yet some can listen to the inner voice with a lot of practice, focus and meditation. This mainly depends on the state of the inner energy, that is, negative/positive, dormant/active and so on.

Sometimes, mind does interfere with the inner voice and that is when the confusion starts. The mind is programmed by what it sees and what has been interpreted, while the inner energy is pure and knows it all. Mind function is very simple. However, the energy within each of us is extremely complex. When the inner energy is in sync with the mind, the decision to be taken is crystal clear without any confusion. Confusion happens when the mind is not in sync with the inner energy.

An attempt has to be made to first align the mind with the inner energy. Since we are exposed to a lot, it needs to be filtered before it settles into our brains and creates havoc. Meditation would help to clear our minds, so any unfiltered thoughts that are not good can be filtered out. The key is to train our minds to be conscious of what it sees and what it absorbs. That is because once an unwanted thought is absorbed it becomes very difficult to filter it out. However, it is possible to clear our minds and remove all the unwanted thoughts, but it would mean more time and effort through meditation.

CHAPTER 11

Love and Believe in Yourself

Many times, we love other things rather than loving ourselves. We admire and adore some people around us; we fall in love with some and willing to go to great lengths to be with them. Sometimes, we are rejected by people whom we most love; this is heartbreaking, and we keep wondering why? We often try to wear branded clothes, good perfumes and spend hours in beauty parlours to look good so that we can be with the person we love the most. However, we are still not able to strike a chord with the people we love the most. Why is that?

The answer is simple. Ask yourself, "We love the people around us, but do we love ourselves enough?" We try to hide behind branded clothes, cosmetics and perfumes to mask ourselves because we do not love ourselves. How do you expect others to love you if you do not love yourself? The energy within us is not comfortable with the feeling of not being loved. So, the energy within us constantly exudes vibrations which are not favourable to attract any other energy around. By not loving ourselves we send out signals to our energy that you are not worth loving.

How can one love others and expect them to believe they love them when they are not capable of loving themselves? It is like a child crying for a mother's love and attention all the time. Just imagine a mother ignoring and not loving her own child! The child would never be happy and do anything to attract the mother's attention. It would get jealous of any other person who tries to get close to his/her mother. The inner energy will not let anyone closer to you, as it would feel lonely from within for not having connected to you.

The energy within us craves for attention. Most of the time, we ignore it and take it for granted. This is true in most of the cases when one does not believe in its own self. They always look out for peace, love, happiness outside rather than looking within themselves. One becomes very uncomfortable in one's own shoes. In that case, how will others feel comfortable with them? For most, it is difficult to love themselves as they do not address the actual issue and try to run away from and not face the real self.

Let me give you some basic examples. I had a friend who hated herself because she was very fat and thought she looked very unattractive. She tried hard to slim down, but eventually gave up as her will power was not very strong. At the same time, she wanted to attract some good-looking guy whom she wanted to spend the rest of her life. To her dismay, she failed to gain the attention of that guy. She tried her best by wearing expensive clothes to take the attention away from her fat body, and also spent hours at the beauty parlour to look attractive. However, all this did not work and things went from bad to worse when she into depression.

I explained that she is not moving in the right direction. Not loving herself was the biggest blunder she was making all along. If her fat body is getting in the way of loving herself and not happy with what she saw in the mirror, then that is the first thing that she needed to tackle. She needed to spend less time in beauty parlours and more time in a gymnasium; she needed to spend less time shopping XXL clothes and more time visiting health stores and eat healthy foods; not spend time running behind guys and start spending time with herself and looking after her own self. Not surprisingly, she took my advice and started to concentrate on her body. I continuously guided and encouraged her to not lose hope midway as the results would take time to show.

Within a year, her weight had dropped by 32 pounds. She looked younger, slimmer, healthier and happier. She loved spending time with herself as she was confident and loved looking at herself in the mirror. She no more hated herself and was very comfortable spending time with herself. She also caught the eyes of good-looking guys and soon married one.

The point I am trying to make here is that one has to love oneself first, and only then we would attract others to accept and love us. Similarly, one has to first believe in one self for others to believe in us. When we believe in ourselves we will give out positive vibrations. This is infectious, and will immediately have people believe in us.

The entire world actually runs on a belief system. If you believe in a product you would buy it; if you believe in a doctor you would take his prescribed medicine; if you believe in the politician you would vote him to be the president/prime minister; if you believe in a religion you would follow it; if you believe in a company you would buy the shares of that company; if you believe that a movie is good you would watch it; if you believe you look good in a particular dress you would buy it; if believe in the person to be your right partner you would marry him/her.

This list could go on and on. To my amusement, most people do not believe in themselves. They strongly believe that they are not capable of doing certain tasks, even if they are capable in reality. Some of them try to perform the task with such hesitation that they are bound to fail. Some of them perform a task with a strong belief they would fail; so much so that their inner energy works towards it to make failure a reality. Yet, some of them never even try due to fear of failure.

Fear, fear and fear is all that most of the people believe in our system. Fear of trying, fear of failure, fear of what people think of them, fear of being hurt, fear of losing wealth, fear of getting noticed, fear of this and fear of that. However, I am not telling you to drive from a mountain top down to a valley nor am I telling you to jump into a well. All I am trying to tell you to do is explore your potential and capability. Do it is all I am saying, with a positive belief in yourself that you can do it.

Yet, one will always find a group of people who would just waste their lives by procrastinating. They dream, they visualise, they know that they have it in them, but yet there is no action. Who can help you if you do not help yourself? Opportunities come and go, but your inaction will do no good to anyone. When confronted, these people promptly reply, "I am waiting for the right time." There is no right time, the time is right now. Start to think, plan and implement your ideas or it would be too late. Have you not heard that the early bird catches the worm?

Most good ideas never see the light of success as they remained just that – ideas, and never planned or implemented. A person would repent after he/she witnesses his/her idea being implemented and turned it into a roaring success. The root cause of not acting on an idea is fear of the unknown followed by laziness to not act upon.

One should not be discouraged by small failures, obstacles or challenges. If one does not experience hardship, how will one become a true winner? After all, there is no fun in achievement if it comes very easily. The journey in itself should be mysterious and enjoyable in order to relish and cherish the final goal achieved.

Our inner energy needs to flow, it needs love, it needs reassurance, it needs to be nurtured, appreciated, and most importantly it needs us to believe in it and have faith in it for us to face any challenges in life. When you believe in yourself, you have a constant company which guides you. It is like having a permanent friend who walks along with you all the time. No matter how you have been performing in life, bad or good, it is always with you and never ceases to love you. It only knows how to reciprocate with abundance. It will never betray you and is always there to help you.

So, start loving yourself! Believe that you can do it and that there is nothing to stop you. No matter what your current status is or what your immediate condition is, great things happen to the ones who *have* the courage to do it with abundance belief in themselves to achieve the ultimate goal and purpose of their lives. Cheers to a good life!

Review

If you are looking out for purpose, peace, love, success and happiness in life, then this book is for you. It tells you how you can uncover the inner energy to help you achieve your purpose and goal in life. The book is full of short stories with messages that can make the concepts more simple and clear for one to understand, relate and practice. The read is easy and enjoyable and touches some very basic principles and guides you to achieve what you dream. It reveals some answers to questions that are frequently asked by most people that science has failed to answer. The techniques explained only help one to achieve his/her dreams with ease. The book encourages you to tap your inner energy to guide you and show you the path to be taken and travelled. The ride is bumpy and the read mysterious, yet the journey is enjoyable and intriguing. It is a life-transforming reading for one and all. So, sit back, relax and enjoy!